ABCs of
Positive Training

A KENNEL CLUB BOOK®

AUTHOR BIOGRAPHY

The author, Miriam Fields-Babineau, with Golden Retriever puppies.

Miriam Fields-Babineau has been training dogs and other animals professionally since 1978. She has owned and operated Training Unlimited Animal Training and Animal Actors, Inc., for 25 years. She teaches people how to communicate with and train their dogs, of any age or breed, specializing in behavioral problem-solving.

Ms. Fields-Babineau has authored many animal-related books, including *Dog Training with a Head Halter* (Barron's Educational Series, Inc.), the e-book *How to Become a Professional Dog Trainer* (Intellectua.com), *Dog Training Basics* (Sterling Publishing Co., Inc.) and many more. She writes numerous articles for trade magazines, such as the award-winning *Off-Lead Magazine* and *Practical Horseman*. She has produced the videos *The First Hello*, which addresses how to prepare a dog for an infant, and *Dog Training with a Comfort Trainer*, which demonstrates how to train a dog using her head-halter design, the Comfort Trainer.

Ms. Fields-Babineau also provides animals for television, film and advertising, having worked with *National Geographic*, Animal Planet, the History Channel, Warner Films, Orion Films, the Discovery Channel, CBS, the Family Channel and many more. When not training other people's animal companions, she travels the country, performing in equine and canine competitions as well as exhibiting the skills of her trained felines.

Photographs by
Bernd Brinkmann, Evan Cohen, Miriam Fields-Babineau, Isabelle Français and Carol Ann Johnson.

KENNEL CLUB BOOKS® ABCS OF POSITIVE TRAINING
ISBN: 1-59378-594-1

Copyright © 2005 • Kennel Club Books, LLC
308 Main Street, Allenhurst, NJ 07711 USA
Cover Design Patented: US 6,435,559 B2 • Printed in South Korea

10 9 8 7 6 5 4 3 2 1

ABCs of Positive Training

By Miriam Fields-Babineau

6. . . . . Simple as A-B-C

11   The Origin of Operant Conditioning

Explore a brief history and development of operant-conditioning methods and meet the pioneers in the field. Take a closer look at the work of B.F. Skinner and see how his research has affected our approach to training dogs and other animals.

15   Reinforcement and Punishment

As you embark on a positive-training program, learn the essentials: different types of reinforcers, schedules of reinforcement, different ways to modify a behavior, the use of correct timing, rewards and how to determine their value to a dog, self-rewarding behavior and different types of punishment.

26   Different Schools of Thought

Look at the different ways of implementing positive-reinforcement training. Explore luring, bridging/rewarding and capturing behavior, or using these methods in combination, to achieve results in a positive manner. Learn about successive approximation and become acquainted with clicker training.

36   Teaching Behavior Both Near and Far

Learn the basics of targeting and the methods used by some of the experts in the field today. You will find out how to teach your dog to target and what equipment is needed.

43   Behavior Shaping

Based on successive approximation, learn how to shape a behavior. Follow the ten key points of behavior shaping as outlined by one of its leading proponents and learn how to practice with a friend so that you'll be more confident when trying it with your dog.

Contents

Loose Leash Walking   50

Learn how to teach one of the hardest lessons to a dog. Vary your method based on the dog's age and attention span, and what rewards he finds valuable. Progress from off-leash in a secure area to heeling on-lead, introducing turns and performing with distractions. Compare the various types of training collars and learn how to prevent pulling.

Sit and Down   68

Using the methods you've learned, it's time to teach two basic obedience commands: sit and down. Learn how to lure into the sit and teach the dog to sit during the heel exercise and for attention. Move on to the down and the special challenges that this command presents; also see how to combine the down with other behaviors.

Stay   82

Teach your dog to stay in the sit and down positions using brief increments of time and gradually progressing. Add movement into the stay, meaning walking alongside and around the dog while he maintains the position. Combine the stay with previously learned behaviors.

Recall and Distraction-Proofing   97

Teach your dog the most important command for him to know and to perform reliably: the recall or come. Increase the distance between you and teach your dog to ignore distractions so that your call takes precedence over his surroundings. Use previously learned behaviors to shape the drop-on-recall.

Positive Reinforcement in Everyday Life   108

Use positive reinforcement for more than just the basic commands. Use this method to house-train your dog as well as to prevent and/or cure common behavior problems, including jumping up, rummaging in the trash, mouthing and chewing, excessive barking, rushing the door and stealing food or other items.

More Sources of Information 124
Index 126

Let's begin by spelling out the terminology commonly used by dog trainers who subscribe to the popular positive-training technique. Positive training is as simple as praising your dog for good behavior—it's as simple as telling him "Yes, Good dog!" and now it's as simple as A-B-C!

ACTIVE SUBMISSION

The dog gives up his leadership role by lying down in a submissive position. He can be lying on his stomach, back or side. His tail is wagging slow and low, and he might be licking his lips, blinking his eyes and holding his ears down. The dog tries to make himself look smaller and less threatening.

ALLEY-OOP

A target training tool designed by Gary Wilkes. It has a circular non-tip base, a cylindrical post about a foot long and a round ball on top of the post. It can be placed on most any surface and remain standing upright, making it a great tool for distance targeting.

AVOIDANCE

Trying to keep away from something.

BAITING

Food or a toy used near the dog's muzzle to attain and maintain the dog's attention.

BEHAVIOR

Anything the dog does is a behavior. Examples: Sit, down, come to you, lick his lips, get into the trash can, jump up.

BEHAVIOR CHAIN

A group of behaviors. Examples: Heel and sit, down and stay, sit and stay then come.

BEHAVIOR SHAPING

Building on the knowledge of a known behavior to turn it into a new behavior. Example: The dog knows how to sit and you wish to teach him to stay. Each time the

dog remains sitting in the same spot for a few seconds longer, his behavior is being shaped to learn how to stay.

BRIDGE

The point between the dog's responding to a stimulus and receiving his reward.

BRIDGING SIGNAL

Examples: The sound of a click, a squeaky toy or the words "Good" or "Yes" in a happy tone of voice, signifying that a reward is coming.

CAPTURING

The moment that the dog has performed a behavior you were seeking, the dog is bridged. This captures the moment that he has done something you wanted him to do. As he has learned that the bridging signal means a reward, he'll seek to repeat the behavior and obtain more rewards.

CLASSICAL CONDITIONING

A stimulus that automatically elicits an uncontrollable response. Example: Pavlov conditioned dogs to salivate when they heard a ringing bell by always feeding the dogs upon the sound of the bell.

CLICKER

A small box, either oval or rectangular in shape. The rectangular box has a piece of metal that, when pressed, makes a clicking noise upon release. The oval type of box has a button that presses upon a piece of metal, making a similar clicking noise upon release.

CONDITIONED RESPONSE

A taught response to specific stimuli.

CONSISTENCY
Doing the same thing every time, regardless of the situation.

CRITERIA
The rules and/or conditions you set that must be met prior to a reward.

DISTANCE TARGETING
Setting up something away from you that you wish the dog to go touch.

DISTRACTION
Anything that takes the dog's mind off of you. Examples: Toys, food, people, dogs, other animals, traffic, loud noises.

DOMINANT
In charge. Number one. The boss.

ELECTRONIC COLLAR/ELECTRONIC STIMULATION COLLAR/E-COLLAR
A collar that will elicit an uncomfortable sensation when triggered either by the vibration of the dog's voice box or the use of a remote-control device.

ESCAPE
Trying to avoid a stimulus. Example: A dog that has learned that a certain object can bring either great pain or anxiety will remain away from that object.

EXTINCTION/EXTINGUISH
To get rid of a behavior.

FIXED INTERVAL
A fixed amount of time after which a reward will be given.

FIXED RATIO
A specific amount of correct responses after which a reward will be given.

FORCE-TRAINED
The dog's being pulled or otherwise made to perform without being given a chance to make the correct choice.

HEAD HALTER
A training tool worn on the dog's head, much like a horse's halter (not a bridle, for there is no bit). The tool is made to apply pressure to the top of the dog's nose and guide the head. The body follows the head, thereby reducing the dog's "pulling" power and quickly teaching him to pay attention in a manner that is understood by the dog.

INSTINCTIVE/INSTINCTUAL BEHAVIOR
A behavior that comes naturally.

LEARNED RESPONSE
A behavior that occurs upon presentation of a specific stimulus. Example: You give the command to sit. Your dog sits. He has learned to respond to the stimulus of your command.

LURING
Using food or a toy to move your dog into a desired position or to elicit a specific behavior.

MOTIVATION
A desire to perform or behave in a specific manner.

NEGATIVE PUNISHMENT
A stimulus or reward is taken away from the dog to extinguish a behavior. Examples: You turn away when a dog jumps on you, not giving him the satisfaction of getting any reaction out of you.

NEGATIVE REINFORCEMENT
An aversive stimulus is removed to encourage a behavior. Example: The pressure of the head halter on the nose is removed when the dog pays attention.

OPERANT CONDITIONING
A signal (stimulus) is associated with a reward, thus eliciting a learned response.

PRAISE
Words of reward spoken to the dog in a high-pitched, enthusiastic tone of voice.

POSITIVE PUNISHMENT
Something is added to punish the dog. Examples: A yank on a neck collar. Spraying the dog in the face with water.

POSITIVE REINFORCEMENT
Something is added to reward the dog. Examples: Praise, treats, toys.

POSITIVE RESPONSE
Your dog behaves in the correct manner.

PREY DRIVE
The drive to go after something that will offer either food, shelter or territory. Dogs are predators and all have this drive. Example: A dog chasing squirrels.

PRIMARY PUNISHERS
A training device. Examples: Choke chain, prong collar, e-collar.

PRIMARY REINFORCER
A reward that the receiver doesn't have to learn to like.

PROGRESSING
Moving forward with training new behaviors.

PRONG COLLAR
A metal linked collar with prongs turned toward the inside, made to be worn against the dog's neck. When tugged upon, the prongs come together in a pinching action, catching the dog's skin between them. Yes, it's painful. However, when used properly, it can be an effective training device for dogs that won't respond to gentler methods. However, these dogs are few and far between, as most dogs will respond to positive training in some manner.

PUNISHMENT
The use or removal of a stimulus to decrease the occurrence of a behavior.

RANDOM INTERVAL
A varied amount of time between actions.

REDIRECTING
Taking the dog's attention away from an improper behavior and turning him toward a proper, or approved, behavior.

REINFORCER
Anything that contributes to the dog's accomplishments.

REGRESSING
Going back a step or two to where the dog was showing successful responses. This happens when progress has stopped; regressing is done in order to maintain a positive attitude.

RELIABILITY
A behavior that is sound and consistent in any situation.

REWARD
Anything the dog likes. Examples: Food, toys, exercise.

RECALL
The dog's coming to you on command.

RESPONSE
Reaction to a stimulus.

SCHEDULES OF REINFORCEMENT
The intervals at which a reward will be given, including fixed interval, variable interval, fixed ratio and variable ratio.

SECONDARY PUNISHER
A correction that is first given concurrently with the primary punisher. Example: The word "No" said in a low, growling tone of voice. The dog will learn to avoid the primary punisher, thus correcting himself upon hearing the secondary punisher.

SECONDARY NEGATIVE PUNISHER
Denying the dog any reaction or reward. This causes the dog to keep throwing out (performing) behaviors, as he hasn't received a reward or punishment of any kind.

SECONDARY REINFORCER
These are actions that the receiver has to learn to like. Examples: The words "Good" or "Yes."

SELF-REWARDING BEHAVIOR
Anything that gives the dog pleasure without your involvement. Examples: Counter surfing, garbage hunting, jumping up, racing through a door.

SHAPING
Building a desired behavior through breaking it down into smaller portions, accomplishing those portions and then bringing them together for the complete desired behavior.

SKINNER BOX
An operant conditioning tool that teaches a small animal (rat, pigeon, chicken) how to obtain a treat by eliciting a specific response. The box is usually made of metal with a food hopper, along with a lighted button or lever that will trigger the food to fall into the hopper when pressed.

STIMULI
Something that triggers a reaction. It can be a target, a lure, a toy or a verbal or visual cue.

SUBMISSIVE
Referring to a dog that wishes only to be part of the pack and not run the pack. He easily submits to a challenge. A submissive dog tries to make himself look small. He will crouch or lie down, show his tummy, tuck his tail between his legs and blink or look away. Some dogs will submissively urinate.

SUCCESSIVE APPROXIMATION
Gradual increase of criteria.

TARGETING
The dog's constantly watching an object or going to it on command.

TERRITORIAL
In charge of a specific space or object.

THROWING OUT A BEHAVIOR
Performing a behavior. A dog that has learned how to elicit rewards will try doing different behaviors to obtain a reward. Example: He sits and doesn't get a reward, he then lies down and doesn't get a reward and he then rolls over and does get his reward. He threw out three behaviors before figuring out the one that was desired.

TOUCHING
A form of positive reinforcement, as dogs adore being scratched in certain places and caressed by their human companions.

VALUE (OF REWARD)
The importance or desirability of a reward to a dog. Each dog has different tastes. Some may think their kibble is the greatest treat in the world, while others will not put forth any effort for something they normally get for free. However, most dogs aren't fed hotdogs, freeze-dried liver, cheese or steak as a normal meal, thus working harder to attain bits of these more sought-after delicacies. To some dogs, food doesn't matter much at all, but touch has a very high value.

VARIABLE INTERVAL
A random amount of time or number of correct responses before a reward is given. The receiver of the reward has no control over when it will be given.

VARIABLE RATIO
Ratio in which the reward is given when the greater amount of correct responses occur within a specific set of stimuli.

VARIABLE REWARD
Changing the value of the reward according to the dog's performance.

VERBAL CUE
The use of your voice to guide your dog and give commands.

VISUAL CUE
The use of body language and specific hand (or other body part) gestures to relay commands or guidance.

Learn how to teach your dog the positive way so that he performs for you anywhere and in any situation.

THE ORIGIN OF OPERANT CONDITIONING

Positive dog training is based upon the studies of noted psychologist Edward Thorndike around the turn of the 20th century. He studied the ability to problem-solve in cats and dogs and was especially interested in the comparison of learned behavior occurring through imitation or observation as well as how quickly a mechanical response was repeated once successful. Do animals learn better through trying over and over and by chance getting the desired response? Or can they learn through watching other animals perform? His results formed a "law" of psychology—the law of effect—essentially stating that the closer the reward to the stimulus, the faster the behavior to obtain that reward will occur, whereas behaviors associated with discomfort will become less pronounced.

A well-trained and well-behaved dog is a wonderful companion who brings so much joy to his owners.

In 1914, John Broadhus Watson extrapolated that Thorndike's law of effect was incorrect and that animals simply respond through instinct and reflex to stimuli, not using any reasoning or problem-solving behaviors. His experiments involved rats in mazes and conditioning them to learn various routes to their food rewards. Watson stated that the reinforcers or rewards might cause a specific behavior to occur more often but didn't act directly on the learning curve. In essence, he rejected the notion of retained memory until a stimulus strengthened the association through repetition.

By the 1920s, Watson's theories were disproved by Edward Tolman, who demonstrated that rats could recognize (through memory) and learn regardless of unexpected changes in the environment, but that decreasing the quality of the reward would weaken the learning. In 1942, this effect was further studied by another behavioral scientist, Crespi, who showed that a decreased reward caused a slower response, while an increased reward elevated the response.

All of this behavioral research was put into perspective when Burrhus Frederic Skinner published *The Behavior of Organisms* in 1938. He connected all of the previous works by stating that the animals were imprinted into responses through sequential learning. The law of effect was resurrected through Skinner's development of the Skinner Box, which enabled psychologists to study the sequence of learned behavior produced over a period of time. Skinner thus developed the basic concept of operant conditioning—operant response (learned response) and reinforcer (reward). The

stimulus was the signal that associated the act with the reward.

In order to fully understand operant conditioning, you'll need to understand how the Skinner Box worked. The box is fully enclosed, with a lever or lighted button on one end, a hopper containing food and nothing else other than a grated floor to stand upon. The subject is an animal such as a rodent, pigeon or primate. The animal is placed in the box and allowed to do as it wishes while inside. A trainer peers into the box via a window and has a finger upon a trigger that releases a food reward.

When food is released, most of the subjects go directly to the hopper and eat the food. If not, the subject will clean itself or walk around, eventually getting to the food and eating it. It quickly learns the food-source location and will remain nearby to obtain more. As it does so, the trainer triggers the release of more food. Each successive reward is given as the subject gets closer to the hopper. Then the subject is required to present a specific behavior to obtain the food reward, such as touching the lever or lighted button. The trainer aims the food release at each successive behavior response that gets the subject nearer to the target

Focused intently on the trainer, these dogs have been conditioned to sit for rewards.

Targeting is the first step in positive dog training.

(lever/button). As the subject becomes conditioned to touching the target to receive his reward, he will increase his targeting responses accordingly, going directly to the target, touching/pressing and receiving the reward. This process is called shaping. The trainer is shaping the behavior through reinforcing each increment of the overall desired response.

In summary, Skinner stated that positively reinforced behavior will recur and that information should be presented in small amounts to shape the responses. He also noted that reinforcement will generalize with similar stimuli and produce secondary conditioning, which means that the learning curve will improve with each successively learned behavior.

Now that you're acquainted with the basic principles of operant conditioning, let's explore how it translates into training our canine companions.

REINFORCEMENT AND PUNISHMENT

The first people to use operant conditioning outside of the laboratory environment were Keller and Marian Breland. They were students of B. F. Skinner during the 1940s. During this time, they used operant conditioning on dogs. Keller Breland was the first to train marine mammals during the 1950s and, soon after, marine park shows were born, such as those at Marineland and Sea World. Operant conditioning is used to this day to deliver to audiences the spectacular dolphin and whale performances seen at amusement parks.

Animal trainers have taken operant conditioning to a more advanced level, pairing it with classical conditioning. Think Pavlov's dog: a bell is rung, which signals food, thus causing the dog to salivate. The dog has learned that the sound brings a food reward. The release of the food reward is preceded by a bridging signal which can be either a light, a buzzer or a clicking sound. The dog learns that a correct response brings the bridge, which signals that the food is sure to come. This allows a trainer to shape multiple behaviors quickly. Here are a few examples of positive reinforcement:

- A dog gets a biscuit for going potty outside;
- You get paid for doing a job;
- A child gets to go to the amusement park for earning good grades;

Marine-mammal trainers use a whistle to bridge the correct behavior.

BELOW: Marine mammals respond well to visual cues.

When a dog jumps up, it's best to not let him get his paws on you at all, as this contact serves as a reward for him.

• A dog receives petting when he jumps up on a person;
• You receive a raise for a job well done.

These examples are all primary reinforcers. A primary reinforcer is a reward that the receiver doesn't have to learn to like. There are also secondary reinforcers. These are actions that the receiver does have to learn to like. Examples are:
• Releasing a tight leash when the dog stops pulling;
• A child is no longer yelled at when his room has been cleaned;
• A cow is no longer shocked (with an electric cattle prod) as long as it keeps moving forward.

Both primary and secondary reinforcers are utilized in animal training as well as in our own everyday lives.

A term with which you should be familiar is "schedules of reinforcement." There are several types of schedules of reinforcement:
• A fixed interval: a reward will be given after a fixed amount of time; for example, every two minutes or every ten minutes;
• A variable interval: a reward will be given but the receiver has no control over when;
• A fixed ratio: a reward will be given after a specific number of correct responses;
• A variable ratio: a reward is given when the greater number of correct responses occurs within a specific set of stimuli;
• A random interval: there is no correlation between the number of correct responses and the receipt of the reward.

Another term with which you should familiarize yourself is "extinction." This is when a behavior has not been reinforced, thereby fading from the repertoire. This is a good means of getting rid of a behavior without having to use punishment, which in itself might encourage a behavior if it is the only means of obtaining attention. An example of this is yelling at a dog for barking, which encourages the behavior by the owner's taking part in the "game." Another example is pushing at the dog for jumping up. The dog is being touched, thereby receiving reinforcement. To extinguish these behaviors (barking and jumping up), they would need to be ignored. Granted, it's difficult to ignore either of them, but the dog's learning that the behaviors no longer bring him pleasure of any kind will eventually extinguish the behaviors.

Skinner defined four possible ways to modify a behavior: positive reinforcement, negative reinforcement, positive punishment and negative punishment. Reinforcement is the use or removal of a stimulus to increase the occurrence of a behavior.

Punishment is the use or removal of a stimulus to decrease the occurrence of a behavior.

Your reaction to a behavior will tell the dog whether or not to continue the behavior. Let's say that your dog is digging in the trash. To him, the reward is getting something to eat, so he will repeat the behavior whenever he gets the chance. However, you can do one of two things to get rid of the behavior: you can either remove the trash can and place it somewhere that Buster can't access it, or you can punish him for the behavior by introducing something aversive, such as a "scat mat." A scat mat has electrical stimulation that will cause the dog's toes to tingle when he steps on it; hence, he'll quickly learn to avoid the scat mat and the trash can.

Removing the trash can is considered negative punishment. This is when something that had

A secondary reinforcer would be the release of the pressure of the leash when the dog stops pulling.

The positive-
reinforcement way
to stop a dog from
digging in the
trash is to divert
his attention, have
him sit and then
click/reward.

been rewarding to the dog is taken away, which will reduce the occurrence of the behavior. The scat mat is considered positive punishment. This is when something aversive is introduced during the behavior that creates enough distress to stop the dog from performing the behavior.

There are other ways to handle the trash-digging pup, and that is through positive reinforcement or negative reinforcement. If you were to divert the dog's attention from the trash can, have him sit instead and then give him a treat, you'd be offering positive reinforcement. If you were to have a leash on your dog and gave it a yank when he went near the trash can, this would be considered negative reinforcement. There are two types of negative reinforcement: avoidance and escape. In avoidance, the dog would steer clear of the trash can when walking in the same room due to the threat of being yanked. In escape, he would run from the room when he even sees the trash can.

Which do you think would be most effective in teaching Buster to stay out of the trash? Actually, it's a combination. Using just one method might cause the dog to get the wrong idea or to become overly frightened of you. The type of conditioner you use depends largely on the dog's personality, the situation in which the behavior is performed and what your ultimate goals are for your pet.

There are several things to consider when using operant conditioning to train your pet.

First of all, you have to make certain that you reward the behavior that you want. For example, if your dog is growling at someone due to fear, the last thing you should do is pick him up and speak in a soothing tone of voice. This reinforces the growling behavior by positive reinforcement and encourages the dog to continue. Instead, negative punishment would be more effective. Using this method, he does not receive attention for his growling; instead, he is not allowed to be with you. Positive punishment might also be more effective. Let's say that when he growled, you squirted him with water. Buster learns that growling earns him a squirt in the face instead of the rewards of being picked up and spoken to in pleasant tones. This will extinguish the behavior.

Another thing you must be aware of when using positive reinforcement is timing. Timing is everything. If you reward your pet at the wrong moment, you will be reinforcing the wrong behavior. For example, you ask your dog to sit. He sits, then gets up. You have not yet taught him to stay and you haven't rewarded him for doing what you asked. He's not sure what to do to earn his reward. If your timing were correct, he would've been bridged (signaled at the moment he sat) and given the reward

It's the rare dog who is not motivated by food, although it does happen. Most dogs have a good food drive and will perform for a tasty reward.

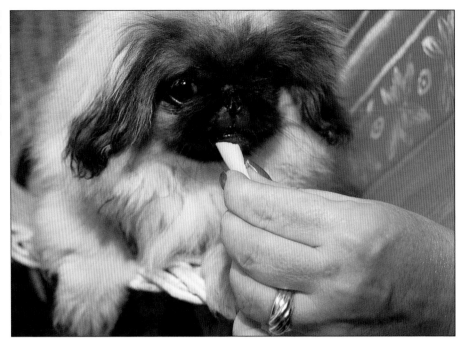

before he got up. This way, he would correlate the sit action with his reward and the behavior would be repeated. Otherwise, he would correlate the action of getting up with his reward and you'd have a dog who has learned to *not* sit. The bridge and following reward need to be done at the very second that the dog does what you've asked of him.

Another factor to consider is the value of the reward. Dogs differ in the values they have regarding what motivates them. Some are happy with a touch or kind words, while others need pieces of hot dog or liver. You'll need to discover what motivates

your dog prior to beginning any training. If your dog likes a number of things, you can vary his rewards according to how well he performs. Let's say you are teaching your dog to sit in heel position. When he sits at your side, but not in heel position, he receives verbal praise but no treat. When he sits a little closer to your side, facing forward, he receives a piece of biscuit. As he learns that better things come to him the closer he sits, he'll sit straighter in proper position. As he achieves his goal, his reward is a piece of freeze-dried liver or hot dog. Buster has learned how to achieve without

The Round Robin game is a great way to involve all family members in the training process, as the dog goes from one person to the next and performs what is asked of him.

your having to force him into it. It would be similar to your getting a better raise at work due to putting in more hours than normal versus a regular raise for merely consistent performance.

A problem with training in this manner is that the animal can learn to associate the reward with only the trainer. He will only listen to or work for this one person. In order for the animal to

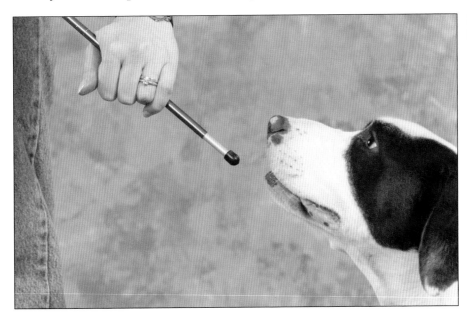

Teaching targeting with a target stick.

This hopeful beggar seems to ask, "Do I get a treat now?"

Puppies have short attention spans and are easily distracted. You will need a reward with high value to the pup to keep his attention focused on the lesson; even at that, you should only work with pups in several-minute sessions.

respond to the entire family, everyone will need to work with Buster. This way, he learns to listen to everyone because anybody in the family has the possibility of being a reward-dispenser. However, when teaching something new and complex, it's a good idea for just one person to be the key trainer so as not to confuse Buster. Once the behavior is learned, others can join in.

If your pet is being rewarded with food, he can become sated. Once sated, he'll no longer be motivated to perform. In order to avoid this, very small pieces of treats should be used, or he can learn to perform for his regular meals. This way, you'll be able to maintain his proper eating habits and weight while he "works for a living" just as he would in the

wild. This would so closely resemble his natural instincts that the dog would feel very fulfilled with his learning process.

Some dogs tire of the same type of food reward, so it would be a good idea to vary the types used. If using freeze-dried liver, try different flavors. If using hot dogs, try different brands or substitute some bacon once in a while. Popcorn is usually a favorite, as are small bits of pizza. As with any treats, dispense in moderation and make sure you choose something that doesn't irritate your dog's digestive system. Inflamed bowels can cause extinction in the behaviors you've achieved, because the dog might learn that the more he performs, the worse he feels.

In order to control when your dog performs, utilize only positive reinforcement when teaching a new behavior during a training session, otherwise your

dog will constantly be bugging you by throwing out behaviors until he receives his reward. At first, the behaviors will be those previously taught, but when he sees that he isn't rewarded for them, the behaviors will turn to negative ones that will ensure him of attention of some kind.

In everyday life with your dog, there are chances of creating what is termed "secondary negative punishers." We tend to do this inadvertently and need to strive to either avoid these situations or turn them into something positive. An example of a secondary negative punisher is calling your dog to come and thus taking him away from something he was enjoying, such as leaving a doggy playgroup or ending a fun game of fetch. While there's really no means of avoiding these situations, you will need to identify them and try to turn them into something positive. So the next time you call your dog to come inside from digging in the yard, think of offering him something that might be more enjoyable, such as eating his meal or doing some tricks for food rewards. Even a tummy rub would be great!

Positive punishment alone can also be abusive if not used correctly. Pairing positive punishment with a secondary positive punisher would be more humane and teaches the dog to

To a retriever, a game of fetch is very rewarding.

correct himself upon hearing the trigger word, such as the word "No" along with a punishment. An example is to say "No" as the dog gets a squirt of water in the face. The dog learns that "No" will coincide with the punishment, thus reducing his bad behavior as soon as he only hears the word. This form of punishment is a very humane means of correcting your dog, although

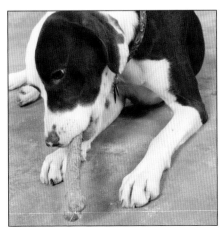

Giving the dog a chew toy to play with is a positive way to end a training session.

there are some schools of thought in which they strive to not punish at all, in which case the undesired behavior may or may not extinguish.

Some dogs learn that while a specific behavior doesn't receive a reward from their human companions, the behavior itself is rewarding. Digging is self-rewarding, as is obtaining scraps from the garbage can. Barking is a fun means of releasing energy. Chewing is a great way to relieve anxiety.

Punishments can also be associated with a specific person. In order for them to work, they must be used by all family members. If the dog has a tendency to do something when nobody is around, he should be contained in an area where he cannot perform the behavior when unwatched. This way, he is conditioned to not behave in such a fashion at any time that he has access to the means of deploying the behavior. An example would be a dog getting on the furniture. Whenever anyone is nearby to see the dog get on the furniture, the dog is corrected for doing so through the use of positive punishment, such as a squirt of water or tug on the leash, along with a secondary punishment, such as the word "No" or "Off." Eventually he'll learn to either avoid the furniture or to get off when the

Digging is an example of a self-rewarding behavior.

secondary punishment is used. However, when no one is around to give the punishment, he gets on the furniture. To condition him out of this behavior, he should not have access to furniture when no one is around to watch him. Eventually the habit will become extinct.

There is also another possible outcome to an animal's behavior and that is no response. There is no reward marker, no "Good Dog," no secondary positive punishment ("No") and no correction. This is considered the "keep going signal," also called the "no reward marker." For dogs that are well into how to throw out (keep performing) behaviors in order to receive their reward, this lack of signal will cause them to continue throwing out behaviors until they get something right. A special word can be formulated to coincide with this lack of signal. Some trainers use "Nope" or "Wrong" or "Try Again." This will cause the dog to try again. However, this will only work with dogs that have been trained via positive reinforcement and have an attention span that will prevent their extinction of performing altogether.

Animals can suffer both physical and mental damage from incorrectly applied punishments and reinforcers. Using these techniques correctly will prevent

If nobody is around to catch him, a furniture-hopper will certainly settle in for some couch time.

harassing or abusing your pet. Be certain that you are clear on the procedures prior to beginning the training process. Try them out on a family member or friend. The children's game "Stop and Go" is a great way to practice, as is the game "Hot or Cold." Things to think about when applying the techniques are: Does it work? If not, why? Was the timing off? Dogs are very forgiving, but once a behavior is learned, it is far more difficult to extinguish it than it is to teach it correctly in the first place.

DIFFERENT SCHOOLS OF THOUGHT

Positive-reinforcement training can be done in several ways. You can lure your dog into position and bridge/reward as soon as he attains what you want, you can capture the behavior by chance or you can wait for him to do something near your objective and shape the behavior into the ultimate goal. Whichever method, or combination thereof, you use depends on what you are teaching, the level of training and how much time you have to accomplish the goal.

Luring can be done with any type of positive reinforcer: food, praise, petting or a favorite toy. Different lures can be used for different situations. Praise is a good reinforcer if the dog did something well but did not improve the behavior, or if the dog is in the process of performing well. Praise encourages the dog to continue the proper response. Touch is a great means of rewarding dogs. They love being stroked and scratched. It's part of pack bonding and

Petting is a great way to praise and reinforce good behavior.

affection display. For dogs that don't care how delectable a food treat might be, stroking can be used as the primary reinforcer. Some dogs love a ball, a rope or a stuffed toy more than a piece of food. The action of giving the dog this toy to reinforce a specific behavior is rewarding and will encourage the dog to continue working. Food, however, is the easiest means of reinforcing good behavior. Most dogs have good food drives and it's just a matter of finding the foods that motivate. Dogs without a food drive will be difficult to teach through positive reinforcement unless you can find another high-value motivator. I've had several dogs

who prefer a tennis ball to food. Give it a try.

For the next method, capturing a behavior, you'll need to be patient and have very good timing. You will need to place your dog in a space or situation in which the behavior you are aiming for will happen at some time or another. An example of capturing a behavior to create a retrieving dog is to bridge/reward when the dog is playing with his toy. At the time he picks up the toy, you want to capture this behavior, so you bridge/reward at that moment. This reinforces your dog's desire to pick up his ball.

Next comes shaping the behavior. This is done in small

Toys can be used as lures to get a dog to perform a behavior.

You will learn through trial and error what your dog values highly as rewards and what doesn't mean that much to him. There's no doubt that this dog relishes time with his toy and retrieving games.

steps. The term is "successive approximation." With each successive successful reaction, you "up the ante" to require a bit more response toward the goal. You captured the dog's picking up the ball; next, you want to teach him to bring the ball to you. You will bridge/reward for each increment. After he picks up the ball, you bridge/reward when he holds it. Then you bridge/reward for his holding it and bringing it part of the way back to you. Each successive increment of covering the distance is bridged/rewarded until he reaches the ultimate goal of bringing the ball to you and placing it in your hand.

To accomplish any form of capture or shaping, your dog will first need to be taught that the sound or sight of the bridge will bring a reward. This can be done one of two ways. He can be lured into targeting or you can merely pair the sound/sight of the bridge with the giving of the reward. Karen Pryor, one of the pioneers of canine operant conditioning, author of *Don't Shoot the Dog* and many other pivotal books on animal training, has termed the start-up process "charging up your clicker" (meaning getting the dog to associate "click" with "treat"). A clicker is a means of bridging a behavior prior to the dog's receiving his reward. The sound of the device is distinct and

The final step in a full retrieve is the dog's releasing the toy and dropping it into your hand.

You can make your dog assume the sit by luring him into position.

ated the click with getting his reward, he will begin throwing out behaviors in order to play the game. Even if you need to work on your timing, your dog will learn. Dogs are very forgiving and can be taught in many ways. However, before you begin using the clicker with your dog, you may want to practice using the clicker to bridge a behavior of a friend or family member. You are better off teaching your dog without confusion. He'll learn faster.

offers a consistent means of signaling a desired response.

If your timing is impeccable, your pet will quickly learn what you want. Once he has associ-

Let's do it! Take your dog to a quiet place where there are no distractions. Be sure he hasn't eaten anything within the last couple of hours. Put your thumb on the movable part of the clicker and wrap your hand around the clicker so that it can't slip out. Hold some small treats in your other hand. Click the

The dog is lured into targeting with a food reward.

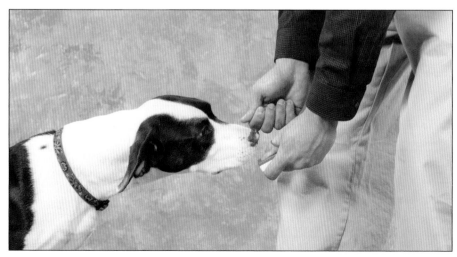

clicker one time and give your dog a treat. Repeat three times (this is the "charging up" part).

By this time, your dog will identify the sound of the click with receiving a treat. He'll start looking at you and getting excited every time he hears the click. If he hasn't identified the sound with the reward, repeat this exercise three more times. Some dogs just take a little longer. If he doesn't respond at all, then you may want to try another type of reward. The dog's not responding means that the reward you are using doesn't have a high enough value to gain your dog's attention.

When repeating this exercise, don't click at a determined ratio, i.e., do not use the same time span between each click. Vary the timing so that your dog doesn't learn a pattern other than the pairing of the click and resultant reward. Be certain not to reward any behavior that you haven't requested.

Now we get into whether to lure your dog into a desired response or just wait for it to occur. This depends on how much time you wish to put into it and what behavior you are teaching. Purists of positive-reinforcement training may choose to wait for something that comes close to the response goal. They'll gradually shape a behavior until it is finally what

they want. This is fine if you are working with an animal that is not used to being touched or spoken to, an animal that doesn't really care about your input as much as just getting that reward. It is an unemotional means of teaching, much like the Skinner Box. This method can also be used when working on an advanced behavior with a dog that is already knowledgeable in the basics and the click/reward system. However, most dogs love touch and praise, so you'll need to add more to the mix to reinforce their behaviors.

Sea mammals and other exotics tend to be taught using this system. They are not acclimated to human interven-

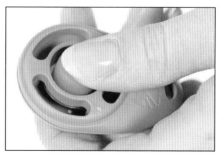

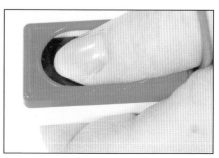

Two types of clicker: the button clicker (TOP) and the box clicker (BOTTOM).

tion and don't care about the sounds and movements we make. All they want is their food. Through time and much patience, they are eventually taught the signals associated with a desired behavior. Teaching them something like targeting or a "go out" signal can take days to months. The trainer has to wait for something close to the desired goal to bridge and reward. Through successive approximation, the exotic animal is taught to target and thus learn more advanced behaviors. Once this animal has knowledge of the routine, he'll learn things at a faster rate, but the initial training period does take a long time. These are the procedures I used when working with sea lions,

polar bears and timber wolves at the zoo. They could not be physically touched, nor could the trainer be particularly close to them while training. When working with the polar bears, I'd be outside their living quarters, separated by two-inch diameter steel bars. These animals are well known for their high prey drive, so I'd rather not be using touch rewards, and they could care less about my voice. I much preferred capturing and shaping the behavior. It may have taken some time, but it was far safer.

Dogs love touch. They love the sound of pleasant voices, and most have very strong prey drives, which will give them incentive to go after the food or toy reward. Clicker training

The basics of positive reinforcement will enable you to build the foundation for higher levels of training, such as for obedience competition.

The dog is behaving politely for examination during a conformation show.

works well when shaping behaviors and rewarding learned behaviors. It is a means of teaching, not a life-long crutch. As dogs learn, they receive secondary reinforcers, such as your praise and touch. These become as much of a reward as the initial click and treat. Where exotic animals must always receive a treat after a specific set of behaviors, it can be phased out in dogs so that they can use their learned behaviors in myriad situations, such as obedience trials, agility and

Learning to navigate the agility course takes time and practice, but is so much fun!

A head halter is a means of humane control when targeting won't work. It should rest comfortably on the dog's face without any jaw restriction.

things within two to five repetitions, but it will also keep you straight on what you are teaching. I've seen some dogs identify the behavior through the command alone after only three, or fewer, repetitions of the exercise.

Dogs can understand many forms of input. A trainer can use positive or negative reinforcement as well as positive or negative punishment. While more traditionally-minded trainers will stick to positive punishment, i.e., using a jerk correction, electrical stimulation, prong collar or other use of something aversive, a positive-reinforcement purist who is knowledgeable in the use of operant conditioning and behavior shaping will use positive reinforcement and negative punishment, causing extinction. Dogs will learn with either means. The difference will be their attitudes when the goals are reached. While some dogs are so forgiving that no matter how they are trained, they still enjoy performing, there are others that will shut down and cower, or hold themselves in active submissive positions while working, showing that they were force-trained or abused while being taught.

search-and-rescue. Sometimes this bridge-and-reward system can be used to overcome bad habits as a redirection tool. However, due to a dog's strong instinctual reactions, it cannot cure everything. There are some situations in which food is not enough of a motivator for a dog to stop a behavior.

In my experience, I have found that dogs learn faster if you pair luring with the use of a bridge/reward. While many trainers will hold off pairing a cue with the action, thus not really teaching a cue until the behavior is learned, I generally teach them both simultaneously. The dog will also learn the cue word and/or visual signal paired with the behavior as you lure him into position. There's no need to hold off on the cue until the dog learns the behavior. Not only do dogs normally learn new

The type of training used depends largely on the dog, the trainer's knowledge and the situation. Positive-reinforcement training is a useful means of starting out with a pup, a shy dog, a friendly dog or a high-drive dog. It may not be useful when starting out with an aggressive or dominant dog. While this type of dog may respond well in some situations, such as in a fenced-in quiet area without distractions, he may not care about food, toys, touch or voice when exposed to a distraction, a stranger or another animal. If your pet displays these tendencies, you should consult with a professional trainer. Using positive reinforcement incorrectly with this type of dog may cause worse problems than it would solve. A professional trainer will know how to properly shape this dog's behavior.

Similarly, once your dog is trained using positive reinforcement, you will need to practice in places other than the quiet training area. New distractions will present a challenge. Another dog might be more desirable than the food or toy reward. Greeting the person walking down the sidewalk might present a higher reward as well. In these cases, you will need to apply a positive-punishment technique in order to regain your dog's attention. This doesn't mean being abusive. Something as simple as turning around to redirect your dog's attention or using the secondary reinforcer word "No" can do the trick. If it does not, you will need to use a head halter or other training device to apply the positive punishment, for doing nothing will not extinguish the behavior.

Be open to whatever your dog requires. There is not any one way to train. Use whatever works. Once your dog understands the routine, you can ease off the luring and you can turn a fixed reward into a variable reward. However, always start at the beginning. In positive-reinforcement training, you cannot begin in the middle. Your dog must first understand the pairing of the bridge with the reward, and then he will identify how to respond to your direction.

The leash attaches to the ring under the chin.

TEACHING BEHAVIOR BOTH NEAR AND FAR

The dog targets on the trainer's hand.

I have already briefly mentioned targeting, which I will explain in more detail here. Targeting is how the animal learns to direct his attention in order to receive his reward. Gary Wilkes, author, speaker, trainer and instructor of trainers, describes targeting as "a process of triggering instinctive behaviors by controlling a dog's focus." It is a fundamental exercise, meaning one cannot train using positive reinforcement without using targeting techniques of some kind. It can be analogized with learning to add and subtract before learning multiplication and division, or building the foundation of a house prior to

putting up the walls. You must have the fundamentals before you can build onto them.

Targeting can be done with luring or it can be done with shaping. Either way, your dog must learn to target in order for positive-reinforcement training to work. It is first taught with the dog close to you and then, using a targeting stick or some other object as a target, at an ever-increasing distance.

I begin targeting using my hand. I hold the treat in my hand so that the dog naturally goes to the scent of the food. As soon as he touches my hand with his nose, I bridge with a

The dog targets on the end of a target stick.

clicker and then open my hand and give him the food. Within a few repetitions, the dog has learned to target on my hand. I can move my hand side to side or up and down and the dog follows, touches and is rewarded. As I teach him to heel, sit or any number of close commands, he will follow my hand target and assume the position required to obtain his reward.

Targeting will need to be utilized when teaching your dog to listen at a distance. Let's say you want him to go to a specific place and sit, to play fetch, to find an object or to go over an obstacle. Distance targeting will need to be done using a target stick and/or an object, because your hand doesn't work well at a distance. You can't immediately reinforce or shape Peanut's distance behavior without first teaching him to target on something that is not attached to you. Also, targeting teaches your dog to focus on something without looking for an immediate treat. The bridge (or click) alone will be enough of a reinforcer to encourage and shape his behavior.

Gary Wilkes has designed several great targeting tools, such as the folding aluminum alloy target stick and the "Alley Oop," a great targeting tool with a yellow base, a black stick and

Equipment for teaching targeting near and far: Gary Wilkes' Alley Oop, a target stick and a treat pouch with treats.

a yellow ball on top. The color yellow is easy for dogs to see. The Alley Oop can be placed anywhere and will not tip over, as the base works much like the "Weebles" toy. (You remember—they wobble, but don't fall down!) That's the Alley Oop. It'll wobble but won't fall over when your enthusiastic Peanut pushes at it. Karen Pryor has designed her own version of the targeting stick. It telescopes from about 5 inches to several feet in length and has a yellow ball at the end for the dog to target on. Terry Ryan, author of *Tool Box for Remodeling Your Problem Dog*, also has designed a similar targeting stick. You

Clicker-training expert Karen Pryor's target stick.

can order these tools online or you can make your own out of half-inch PVC with some black liquid latex or tape on one end.

You're probably trying to hold all of these things in your hands and wondering how you're going to hold treats, a clicker, a target stick and possibly a leash. What, you weren't born with four hands? Fear not, there is a technique to this juggling madness.

Using your dominant hand (left if you're a southpaw like me, right if you're like most people), circle your thumb and forefinger around the end of the target stick. Stick the clicker between the stick and your fingers, placing your thumb on the clicker in the proper location to make it click. Rotate your wrist so that the target stick is pointing down, toward the dog. Your treats should be in a pouch, allowing easy access. Your leash is held in your free hand; however, if you are doing target-stick training, it means that most likely your dog has completed his basic obedience and is now working on off-leash training. For all off-leash exercises, make sure you are in an enclosed area where your dog cannot escape or become distracted. A safely enclosed area is recommended regardless of your dog's training level. Following this policy will free up a hand to grab a treat instead of holding the leash. *Voila!* All with only two hands.

Some dogs might be frightened of a suddenly-appearing target stick. This doesn't necessarily mean that they were beaten with sticks, only that they are unfamiliar with them. Unsocialized dogs aren't afraid of other dogs or people because they are afraid of being bitten or beaten; rather, they are afraid due to lack of exposure. You will need to slowly acclimate your dog to the target apparatus. Do the following:

How to hold the clicker and the target stick in the same hand to leave your other hand free for dispensing treats.

1. Lay down the tip of the target stick and place some food near it. As your dog investigates, click and allow your dog to eat the food.

2. Lay the food closer and closer (shaping your dog into going closer to the target stick).

Click each time he reaches the food.

3. Put the food directly on the end of the stick, which you wish Peanut to target. Again, click when he touches it.

4. Lift the tip of the stick slightly off the ground. When Peanut investigates and sniffs the end of the stick, click and give him the treat.

5. Gradually lift the stick higher with each successive exercise, clicking and rewarding for each correct response.

Another means of acclimating your dog to the stick is to fold it up (or slide it closed) and allow only a small piece to stick out of your hand. Guide your dog into targeting on your hand. As soon as he touches your hand, click and give him his reward. The next time, make certain that his nose touches the target stick. As he learns that the stick is the point at which you wish him to target, you can begin sliding it out of your hand and making it longer with each successive request, which in turn teaches your dog to target upon the end of the stick instead of your hand. You can test his responsiveness to the stick by moving it side to side and up and down. Each time your dog touches the end of the stick, click and reward.

If at any time your dog makes an incorrect response,

You will want to have your treat pouch and clicker handy during all training sessions.

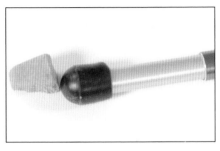

To teach targeting on a stick, lay the tip of the target stick on or very close to a treat.

such as coming to you for the food or sniffing the ground, take the target stick away and say "Wrong" or "Uh, uh" in a tone that doesn't carry inflection. You want the dog to continue trying, so you don't want to use a low tone of voice, which signifies that he is doing something rong. Instead, you want to use the word as an extinction cue, to extinguish his incorrect response and redirect him to the correct response. Gary Wilkes describes the tone as "informative, not discouraging."

Now that Peanut will touch the target stick, you can begin teaching him to touch other objects on command. Pick an object, such as a specific toy,

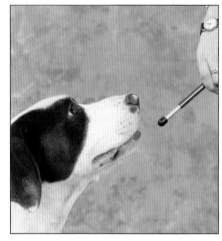

Begin by exposing only a short length of the target stick so that the end is still close to your hand.

As your dog learns to target on the end of the stick, gradually increase the length of the stick.

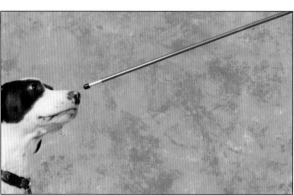

Eventually, you will be able to expose the full length of the stick.

the Alley Oop or a spot on a fence. Put the tip of the target stick on the spot or object and give the command "Touch." As your dog has learned to touch the tip of the target stick, regardless of its location, he will go to touch it. When he does so, he'll be touching both the target you chose and the stick. Click and reward as he does so. Be sure to add the word "Good" or "Yes" as he performs correctly. Keep in mind that this reinforcing word is a secondary reinforcer that will be used throughout his life to mark a correct behavior, whereas the clicker will be phased out. Pairing the word with a positive response is very important.

After you have repeated this exercise eight to ten times, your dog has been conditioned to go to the object to which you are pointing. Next, step back a foot or so and hold the target stick out of sight as you say "Touch." Your dog will not see the target stick but has been conditioned to go to the object you had previously targeted with the stick. He will go toward the object. As soon as he moves toward the object, click and reward. Each increment closer, click and reward. When Peanut touches the object, be sure to make a big deal out of his response with a happy "Yes!" as you click and reward. Your dog has now learned to target on something other than a target stick, at a distance from you. You can teach him to target on anything, gradually increasing the distance with each success. Not only have you taught your dog to target, you have also taught yourself how to shape a behavior.

ABOVE: Double targeting is a means of transferring the target goal; for example, from your hand to the Alley Oop. LEFT: A general touch on the Alley Oop is good when starting to teach the dog to target on it.

"What's next?" Positive training methods will produce a dog that enjoys his lessons and is eager to learn.

Behavior Shaping
A Guide to Getting What You Want

If you have been successful in teaching your dog to target, you have already learned the basics of behavior shaping. The key words are "successive approximation." With each successive success, the criteria are increased. When you taught your dog to target, you began by pairing a treat with a click. Or you began by luring him into position, bridging with a click or praise and then giving him the treat. You moved your target, Max followed, he received the bridge and reward. You gradually taught him to target on another object, first nearby and then at a distance.

Karen Pryor has outlined "Ten Laws of Shaping" a behavior. Following this code will help you teach your dog just about anything through positive reinforcement.

1. *Raise criteria in increments small enough so that the subject always has a realistic chance of reinforcement.*

For teaching the dog to target, you began by pairing the food with the touch of the target. To increase the criteria, you moved the target a short distance away from the dog. Each time he accomplished this, you increased the distance or changed the direction. You taught Max to target in small enough increments to make sure that he was successful.

2. *Train one aspect of any particular behavior at a time. Don't try to shape for two criteria simultaneously.*

You first taught Max to target on the stick before teaching him to target on

By following the treat in the trainer's hand, the dog is lured into the sit position.

Hand targeting in the sit position facing the trainer.

another object. You could not have been successful trying to do both at the same time. It would have confused your dog.

3. *During shaping, put the current level of response on a variable-ratio schedule of reinforcement before adding or raising the criteria.*

To insure your dog is knowledgeable in touching the target, make him touch it several times (and click) prior to giving him his reward.

4. *When introducing a new criterion, or aspect of the behavioral skill, temporarily relax the old ones.*

If you first taught your dog to target on your hand and wish to teach him to target on the stick, you'll need to reduce or relax the hand target by only reinforcing him when he touches the stick. There's no need for a correction if he touches your hand, just don't reinforce it. He has to figure out the response you are looking for and this may take a period of trial and error.

5. *Stay ahead of your subject. Plan your shaping program completely so that if the subject makes sudden progress, you are aware of what to reinforce next.*

When teaching your dog to target on the stick, you gradually increased the criterion from placing the food directly

An attentive expression means that your dog is ready to respond.

on the end of the stick to giving it to him after he touched it. You planned your incremental criteria by knowing where you were going with it.

6. *Don't change trainers midstream. You can have several trainers per trainee, but stick to one shaper per behavior.*

Each person has his own way of doing things. If Max is

on a roll, the last thing you want to do is to confuse him by changing the environment during his initial training progress. Switching the person who is doing the shaping is a huge change.

7. *If one shaping procedure is not eliciting progress, find another. There are as many ways to elicit behavior as there are trainers to think them up.*

One dog might learn quickly by simply pairing a click with the giving of the reward, while another will learn faster through luring into position and then bridging/rewarding. Dogs respond to many different training methods.

8. *Don't interrupt a training session gratuitously; that constitutes a punishment.*

Always end a training session by doing something fun. If your dog loves to play fetch, do a couple of rounds with him. If he likes having his tummy rubbed, do so. Always signal the end of a session by doing something positive.

9. *If behavior deteriorates, go back to kindergarten. Quickly review the whole shaping process with a series of easily earned reinforcers.*

It is better to regress in order to progress. If Max isn't learning something at a specific level, go back a step or two, ensuring that

A tummy rub is a great way to end a training session.

You might end your training session with a game that your dog enjoys playing with you.

the training remains positive. He may not have actually learned something required to continue forward. Backing up will return to the point where your dog was successful, thereby maintaining the positive response and attitude, retaining Max's attention and drive. Rebuild the behavior and then go on to the next step, keeping the goal small.

10. *End each session on a high note, if possible; in any case, quit while you're ahead.*

Make certain that your dog provides a correct response before ending a session. If he shows signs of getting tired, end the session quickly by doing something he is sure to perform.

A great way to practice shaping a behavior prior to trying it on your dog is to enlist the help of a family member or friend. You'll play the shaping game with them first in order to perfect your timing and shaping plan. Start with the person in the middle of a room. Make your goal to have the person touch a nearby piece of furniture with his left hand. You tell the person that each time you click, he is doing something that you want:

• When the person is facing the direction of your chosen piece of furniture, click;
• When the person takes a step in the direction of the furniture, click;

• When the person takes another step in the direction of the furniture, click...and so on, until he reaches the furniture;
• If the person by chance raises a hand, click;
• The next click is if the person raises his left hand;
• The following click is if the person raises his left hand and brings it toward the furniture;
• When the person touches the furniture with his left hand, click;
• When the person lays his hand on the furniture, click.

Now the person has accomplished touching the furniture with his left hand. Give that person a piece of chocolate, as the behavior has been shaped. The next time that person wants you to give him a piece of chocolate, he will touch that piece of furniture with his left hand. Just kidding....people know better! He will get the chocolate for himself! There's not much you can do about counter-surfing people, but there's a lot you can do with counter-surfing dogs.

Now that you have an idea of how to shape a behavior (after all, you've done it with teaching your dog to target and with a person), try using this technique to get your dog into performance condition. Shape an obedient dog.

Positive training produces a positive attitude and a happy dog.

LOOSE LEASH WALKING

Teaching Ranger to walk on a loose leash is probably one of the most difficult behaviors to teach. Most people have a habit of holding the leash tightly or pulling back whenever the dog pulls away. This makes the dog pull harder. Any leash that applies constant tension will teach the dog to pull away. It's a natural reaction. A dog's instinctual tendency to pull might be more developed in the working breeds, but is intrinsic in all breeds. Huskies, Malamutes and Samoyeds are specifically bred to pull sleds and thus have a stronger instinct to pull, but your little Pomeranian can do the same, especially considering that he is derived from these Nordic breeds. A Yorkshire Terrier will pull, as will a Cocker Spaniel. You apply pressure, the dog returns it.

The key to teaching your dog to not pull on the leash is to not apply pressure. Instead, teach him to pay attention. Teach him how much more fulfilling it is to

Off-leash heeling is at the higher levels of training and is an exercise in obedience competition.

walk at your side than to run to the end of the leash, get pulled on and strain to greet the other dog and his owner walking toward you. You'll have to offer the better choice. You'll have to condition Ranger to prefer the correct response.

The method you use to train Ranger to heel depends largely on his age. It also depends on your ultimate goals. Do you want him to perform in obedience trials or just to walk with you around the neighborhood? You'll have to define your goals prior to starting your training. You'll need to communicate to your dog when you wish for him to pay attention and when he's allowed to sniff and investigate an interesting trail. Ranger will need to listen, regardless of where he is and what is going on around him. He'll need to do so on one command. Set your parameters and stick to them.

Once you have set your goals, you'll need to plan your shaping routine. Remember that you must stay a step or two ahead of your dog. If he accomplishes several steps very quickly, you'll need to move on to the next step. If he seems to lose the ability to perform at a specific level, you'll need to go back a step or two to return to a level at which he is responding properly. There are no set procedures for accomplishing any single

behavior, only a means of gradually shaping a response into your ultimate goal. Be flexible. Be consistent. Be persistent. Be patient. Praise a lot and keep everything fun and positive.

TRAINING A PUPPY (FIVE WEEKS TO FOUR MONTHS OLD)

Puppies may have short attention spans, but they learn quickly and eagerly. They are very attached to their pack members and tend to remain close by, which makes teaching them to be attentive relatively easy. The younger the pup, the easier it is to gain his attention. As the pup gets older, three months or more, the distractions in the environment may take precedence if you haven't already taught him that being attentive is more attractive.

At this stage, you don't want to work on the leash. Yes, we are starting off-leash training (in your enclosed area) before attempting on-leash training. This will allow you to concentrate on attaining the appropriate response from your pup without having to fiddle with the leash as well. Once puppy has an idea of what to do, you can add the leash.

Puppies tend to have a high food drive. It is their primary incentive. I have found that luring a pup into a behavior is the fastest means of achieving

Use a food lure to attain the pup's attention.

time-consuming, and many dog owners haven't the patience or time to begin this way. Besides, pups love to hear their owners' voices and feel their owners' touch. This more personal approach makes it more enjoyable for the puppy.

The first training sessions should be done in a place with which the pup is familiar. He has already explored the surroundings and there aren't any distractions. Hold the treat in one hand and the clicker in the other. First teach puppy to target. Put the treat under his nose to gain his attention. As soon as you have his attention, click/praise and give the treat. Move the target slightly to one side. As puppy

goals. As the pup is lured, the clicker can be added. To some, this may be backwards. Some trainers would prefer to begin by using the clicker and gradually shaping the behavior. I find this

Two pups can target at the same time on the same target.

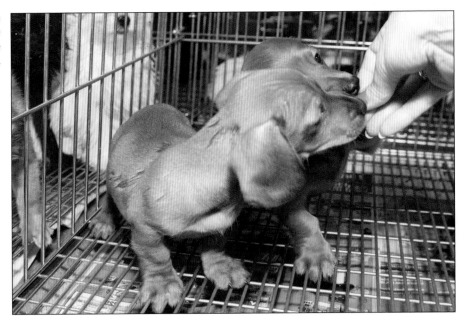

All dogs, big and small, young and old, should be taught to heel.

follows, click/praise and give him the treat. Move the target slightly to the other side. Again, as puppy follows with his nose, click/praise and give him the treat. Repeat with a slight up and down motion. As he follows your hand, click/praise and give the reward. You now have puppy targeting! In the few minutes it took to teach your puppy to target, he learned a couple of new behaviors as well as the meaning of your bridge (click/praise) and that following his nose brings great rewards.

Give puppy a break for a couple of minutes. You'll need to identify this relaxation time in some manner. Begin by using a specific word, such as "Break,"

"Release," "Free time," etc. As soon as you utter the relaxation cue word, pet your pup. The action of petting distracts him from the targeting routine because pups love being touched. It's a great reward and a positive means of ending a training session.

Puppies tend to perform best when you work in short time spans. Perhaps ask for three to five responses and stop, or work for a minute and a half and stop. This will maintain pup's attention span for an overall longer period of time. He will want to continue, deepening his desire to perform.

Now that you have pup's attention on your hand (make

Keep the target in the location where you wish your puppy to work.

will he go crazy over? What toy will he do anything to get? Use a valuable motivator. If puppy wants the reward, he'll do anything to get it and thus learn at a fast rate.

Now that you have puppy's attention at your leg, take one step forward on the leg that he is targeting and give the command word that you wish to use for the exercise, such as "Walk," "Heel," or "Let's go." As he moves with you, following his target, click/praise, stop and reward.

The next level is taking two steps as puppy follows your target. Click/praise and reward as

Begin walking on the leg closest to your dog.

certain it's your left hand if you want him to walk with you on your left side and your right hand if you want him to walk with you on your right side), bend down and place your hand near your calf. As puppy follows your hand, click/praise and reward him when he touches it with his nose; he will do so fairly quickly. If not, lure him there by allowing him to sniff your hand and then slowly bringing your hand to your lower leg.

If your pup doesn't seem to be interested in the treat, you may need to try something else. Remember that one of the first things you should do, prior to training, is discover what "drives" your puppy. What food

he remains at your side for two steps. Each successive time that you tell your puppy to heel (or whatever word you are using), add another step. Within a few minutes, you'll be walking eight to ten steps or more. Give your pup a break for a few minutes and then repeat the exercise, starting at 5 steps and working up to 15. Take another rest period and begin again at 10 steps, shaping your way up to 20.

Once puppy is heeling nicely, begin incorporating turns. Step forward five steps or so, then turn right, stop, click/praise and reward. Repeat at least three times. Then go forward a variable number of steps, turn, stop, click/praise and reward. The next time, add a few steps beyond the turn prior to bridging. Do the same with a left turn. Start to vary which turns you do and the amount of steps prior to and after the turns. Be sure to give your pup a break every three to five minutes. If he starts to show signs of disinterest, i.e., sniffs at the ground, looks away or gets droopy, stop, but always end on a good note with baby Ranger performing an exercise correctly.

As puppy picks up on the routine, you can begin decreasing the baiting/luring procedures. Gradually lift the target higher and start to stand up straight. (You can only walk hunched over for so long!) Provided that puppy maintains the proper trajectory (remaining in heel position), praise as he remains in position and click again upon stopping. Now that he isn't receiving the reward as often, the click and praise are reinforcing his behavior. The click should be used as a cue to signal the end of an exercise.

TRAINING THE ADOLESCENT DOG (FOUR MONTHS TO TWO, POSSIBLY THREE, YEARS OLD)

Training a dog at this age is probably the most challenging time. Dogs of this age are in the process of establishing their place within their families, are easily distracted and are full of energy. Adolescent dogs are no longer glued to their pack

Before any on-leash training can begin, the pup must be accustomed to wearing his collar.

Using a head halter, if done properly, gives you instant control in all situations.

members; they'd rather be out and about, exploring new territory and testing their potentials.

You can try starting out with the same procedures that you'd use with a young pup, but they won't work when your dog is exposed to distractions of any sort. They also won't work if the dog is trying to assert dominance. In fact, it will be difficult to use purely positive reinforcement at this time. You will need to also use some punishment now and then in the form of positive punishment (pressure of a head halter and leash) and negative punishment (taking away something positive), and the secondary punishing reinforcer, the word "No."

Note: You'll notice throughout this book that I never suggest the use of negative reinforcement. This is akin to putting your dog in a cage that has an electrified floor, such as those used in early behavioral research to test the use of aversives in learning. A rat or monkey was put in the cage and a shock was administered to either shape or extinguish a behavior. I cringed when I read about it, and I am much against the use of negative reinforcement in any training process. While electric-shock techniques are more extreme than what a pet owner would use, I still do not recommend any type of negative reinforcement.

Just so teenage Ranger gets an idea of what you want, begin by working with him in a quiet area without distractions. Be sure to use a reward that he'll go bonkers over. It has to have a very high value to maintain his attention. In my experience, I have found freeze-dried liver to work very well, as well as small pieces of hot dog or cheese. Make sure that whatever you use won't upset Ranger's tummy! These high-value treats are very rich foods and a dog with a sensitive stomach can have a bad reaction to eating too many of them.

Teenage Ranger may not require baiting/luring into position. Due to the adolescent's higher energy level, you can probably shape the entire behavior into existence. However, if you want to progress faster, use a lure. You can always phase it out as you go.

Begin with charging up your clicker. Teach teenage Ranger to connect the sound of the clicker with receiving a reward. He should have the idea after three to five tries. Now, to shape the heel position:

1. When your dog looks at you, click/praise and give the reward. (If you are using a lure, show him the reward and allow him to come for it. As he does so, click/praise and reward.)

2. When he takes a step

To start the dog walking beside you, take a step forward as you show him the target.

toward you, click/praise and give the reward.

3. When he takes two steps toward you, click/praise and give the reward...and so on, until he is near you.

Turn so that Ranger is at your side. As soon as he's in the correct position, even if you have to put him in the position, click/praise and reward. If he remains in position, click/praise again and reward. As he continues to remain in position, bridge and reward. If he moves, don't do anything, just wait. When he puts himself into heel position, click/praise and reward. If he fails to put himself into heel position, lure him there with the bait and then click/praise and reward.

Now start adding the heel command. Say his name and then the command word. One time. Never repeat your command or it just becomes background noise that your dog learns to ignore. It has no meaning if you don't explain what happens when the command is stated. Give the command as Ranger places himself in or maintains the heel position.

Holding the reward on your leg, just out of his reach, is also a great means of explaining what you want. The lure will put him into position without your physically having to do so. It's

far faster than just waiting for the behavior to occur.

As soon as teenage Ranger puts himself into position, click/praise and reward. Continue to praise as he remains in position. Next, take a step forward as you say "Ranger, Heel." Lure with the food. As he remains in heel position at your side, praise. If he doesn't remain in position, then lure him into position with the bait. Always praise when Ranger attains the position you've requested.

Once you are able to take more than a couple of steps and teenage Ranger remains at your side, praise him as he maintains his place. Click and reward when you stop, signaling the end of the exercise. This doesn't necessarily mean a release or break time, just the end of that heeling moment. You can give him the command again after his reinforcement and continue on.

Gradually shape teenage Ranger into a heeling machine. Turn a couple of steps into 3, 4 and so on until you can move forward 20 steps or more, turn left, turn right and vary your pace. Give him a break every five minutes or so and pet him and/or play with him. This way, you are ending the exercise with something positive.

Now it's time for working with distractions. Most adolescent dogs will try to pull away, sniff interesting scents and jump around. They are teenagers! They have lots of energy. Allow your teen to blow off some steam prior to training. Play fetch, race around an enclosed area with him, anything to take the edge off. Your teenage Ranger can't concentrate if he doesn't receive enough exercise.

When confronted with distractions, many adolescents could care less about food or toys. They'd rather investigate, race after or otherwise engage the distraction. Without having a means of applying positive punishment, you don't stand a chance of regaining his attentiveness.

To use a positive punishment successfully, you will need to review procedures for their appropriate use. Whatever you use, whether a martingale collar, head halter, choke chain, prong collar or electronic collar, you will need to make sure that you are using it correctly. These are all unique tools that require skill to use or they can become abusive.

For anything that goes around the neck, you don't want to maintain constant pressure. The

pressure against the dog's trachea will do two things: collapse the trachea and cause the dog to become more adamant about pulling. Therefore, the martingale collar, choke chain and prong collar should never have constant pressure applied. In other words, never pull! Tug and release. Turn and redirect. Use sparingly, only when absolutely necessary.

An electronic collar is not used to restrain a dog. It's used as positive punishment. When the dog doesn't respond to redirection, positive reinforcement or negative punishment (taking away something he likes), you'll need to use something that gets his attention. Again, this device can easily be abused, so be sure that you are well versed in its use prior to putting it on

The martingale collar.

your dog. The electronic stimulation needs to be applied at the very moment that the dog is misbehaving. He'll immediately need to be redirected toward a good behavior and rewarded for doing so.

Head halters offer a means of controlling the dog without using pain as a reinforcer. Instead, the pressure on Ranger's muzzle acts as a means of communicating that he's done something wrong. Dogs will put their mouths over the muzzles of other dogs to show dominance or correction. The head halter simulates this behavior. Head halters also

reduce a dog's pulling power by up to 90%, for dogs must follow their heads. For some dogs, the head halter is a "magic pill"; for others, it's just a pill, for they fight the feel of the apparatus on their faces. I have found that Labrador Retrievers in particular tend to dislike the feel of a head halter more so than other breeds. Many dominant dogs will try to get the head halter off, while overly submissive dogs may totally shut down over being so overwhelmingly dominated. Head halters aren't for all dogs, but they do work on about 80% of dogs to stop pulling behaviors

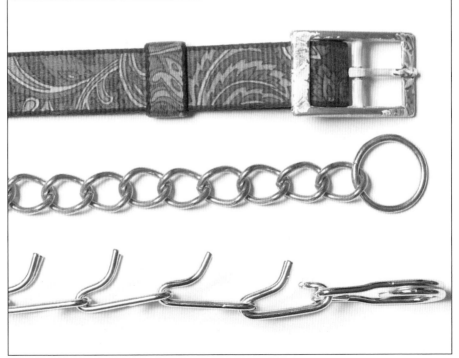

Three types of collar: the nylon buckle collar on top, the choke chain collar in the middle and the prong collar on the bottom.

Close-up of the head halter. This training device offers a means of controlling the dog without using pain as a reinforcer, but you must be shown how to use it correctly.

and overcome many forms of aggression. This tool will also be invaluable in training dogs that have no food or toy motivation.

Keep in mind that all of these training tools should be used sparingly and in a manner to redirect the dog into appropriate behavior. Once Ranger is paying attention, even for a second, click/praise and reward. As this happens, you will successively require a longer and longer moment of attentiveness as well as more and more response through shaping it. Do your research or go to training lessons prior to using any training tool with which you are unfamiliar. The aim here is positive-reinforcement training, not abusive training.

TRAINING OLDER DOGS (OVER THREE YEARS OF AGE)

The method you use for a dog over three years old depends largely on the dog. Each dog is an individual and each will respond to his environment differently. Temperament testing prior to training will help you understand which track to take. Whatever the track, it can all be turned into a means of training using positive reinforcement.

Temperament testing is often used on shelter dogs and rescued dogs. It is also done with pups to discover their future potentials. The temperament test you do on your older dog doesn't have to include personality-trait issues, only ease-of-training issues. Most older dogs will have a good food drive, for they aren't as easily distracted by other animals, people and toys. They've had time to acclimate to their environment and might socialize on a regular basis. They don't have as high an energy level as teenage Ranger. Ask yourself these questions:

1. Does my dog have a food he loves? If so, what is it?

2. Is my dog allergic to any foods? If so, stay away from them and try something he both likes and can handle.

3. Does my dog enjoy interacting with me?

4. Does he follow me around?

5. Is he curious?

If your dog loves food, that makes using positive reinforcement easy. If he likes to follow you around, enjoys your touch and thrives on praise, he's a sure thing. If he's curious, he'll learn quickly and there'll be no stopping him from becoming a genius. Here are some more things to discover more about your dog's personality and future ability to learn using positive-reinforcement training.

To test a dog's attentiveness, think about the following: If your dog likes to lick you, touch you and follow you around, he's an ideal candidate for positive-reinforcement training. If your dog likes to sleep in a room away from you and comes to you for touch only when he feels like it, but does come to you when you call him, he's still a good candidate. If he doesn't listen at all and moves away from you, you most likely

An ideal candidate for positive-reinforcement training is a dog who loves to show affection.

Praise helps to maintain your dog's attention.

When your dog pulls on the leash, "be a tree." Don't move!

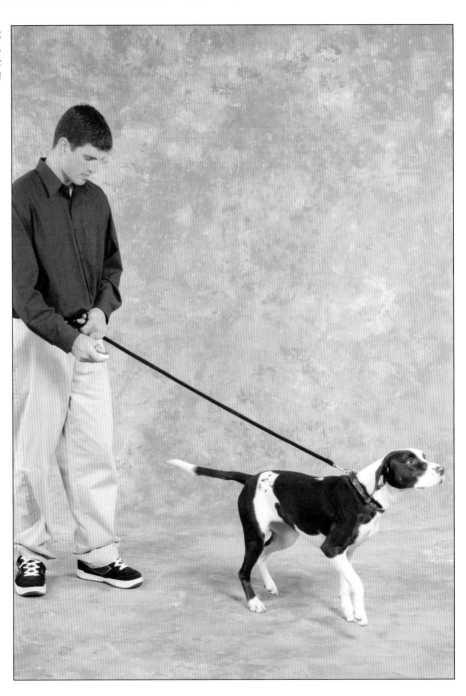

won't be able to use just positive reinforcement; you might need some positive punishment as well. Wait and see. Don't start off with positive punishment, but be ready to use it if necessary.

Most dogs have some sort of prey drive. They'll run after moving objects or at least look at them. They enjoy their meals and they like to go for walks. A dog that will perform well with positive-reinforcement training has a good work drive, too. He loves to be active and interactive. A dog that is interested in both his environment and in where you (the trainer) are in relation to his location will be a good candidate for positive-reinforcement training. A dog that would rather go after moving critters and objects can still be a good candidate, but you might need to use a positive-punishment training tool to control him when distracted.

A dog that doesn't care where you are or what you are doing, and/or is aggressive, will need to be trained with a positive-punishment tool, most notably a head halter or electronic training device. Using a neck collar on this dog will result in more aggression and future problems.

For the dog that is responsive and attentive, and has good drive, begin training as you would a teenage dog or a pup. He'll respond quickly. When he is

successful in an area without distractions, gradually increase the distraction level until he is proficient with anything you request. For the dog that is still easily distracted, overly friendly with newcomers or just boisterous, use a positive-punishment device when needed. Most likely, you'll need it when starting with distraction work, but can soon phase it out.

For the dog that is more assertive and doesn't care about food, touch and praise rewards, you'll need to train with a head

Lure the dog back to your side, then click and reward.

halter and reward him with praise and touch at the very moment he is behaving correctly, even if that moment is only a fraction of a second. Let him know how much nicer your response is when he provides the behavior you requested. You'll soon discover that this dog is becoming more attentive and calmer, and he is developing more of a work drive as he extinguishes his inappropriate behavior.

Here are a couple of ways that you can change pulling into watching:

1. The Be a Tree exercise: When Ranger rushes ahead of you, stand still. Don't let the leash out. When he looks back at you, click/praise and reward. If he remains looking at you or looks at you a second time, click/praise and reward. When he takes a step or two toward you, click/praise and reward. As he moves closer and closer to you, click/praise and reward. When he returns to you, click/praise and reward. Take another couple of steps forward. If Ranger again rushes ahead, do the same exercise of shaping his return. If Ranger remains with you, click/praise and reward.

2. The Turn and Redirect exercise: This is most useful when using a head halter. When Ranger rushes ahead, apply a smooth downward pull as you turn right. Stop. If Ranger is at your side, click/praise and reward. If not, again apply a smooth downward pull and turn. As soon as Ranger is at your side, click/praise and reward.

3. The Bump and Turn exercise: When Ranger is just starting to pull ahead, take a big step forward with your right leg and bump him aside with your left leg as you turn left. Dogs hate being bumped and this positive punishment will quickly teach Ranger to pay attention to you as you walk. As soon as he slows down and looks at you, click/praise and reward.

In time, the only response you'll have to give is praise, but this takes months, if not years, to achieve. Repetition. Repetition. Repetition...and loads of praise!

When using a head halter, apply a smooth downward pull as you turn.

Use your left leg in front of the dog while turning left to halt his forward momentum.

Sit and Down

The easiest means of getting started with placement of the sit and down positions is to use a food lure. Once the dog is lured into position, you can click/praise and reward. Sounds easy, right? It should be, but then our dogs aren't robots. Dogs are as individual as humans. Each dog will respond to cues differently. Not all dogs are driven by food rewards. Some will prefer touch, verbal praise or a special toy. Others don't care about any positive reinforcers!

First, I'll start by discussing how to teach your dog to attain the sit position through luring and reinforcing with clicking, praise and a food reward. I will follow by communicating to the dog by using a toy, then through touch. Another thing: if you have taught your dog to target with the stick, you can use it as a means of luring into position as well.

Now we'll talk about luring with food. Most dogs follow their noses. To lure Butch into position, you need only put the

One way to achieve the down is to capture the behavior by clicking when your dog lies down on his own.

food in the right spot, and click/praise and treat as soon as he attains that position. The tricky part is knowing where to place the treat. When luring Butch into a sit, you'll want to place your lure directly between his eyes, just a few inches out of reach. He'll try to reach the food by looking upward. As he looks upward, his rear end will lower. As he does so, even just a little, click/praise and give him his treat. If Butch didn't do a full sit on the first try, that's okay. Repeat the exercise and request just a little more the next time.

Some dogs may need a helping hand, as they are so excited about the exercise that they just can't sit still at all. As an aid to overanxious Butch, gently press his rump as you lure his nose upward. Click/praise and reward at the very second that his rump touches down. You may need to aid him a few times, but he'll catch on.

After a few go-rounds, or even at the beginning because the dog usually learns the position quickly, add the actual command "Sit" to your cues. Tell him "Butch, Sit" as you place your lure over his head and between his eyes. Give him a "Good dog" as he attains the position and you click and give him the treat.

Now onto luring with a toy,

Click as your dog sits.

which is rather similar to luring with food. The difference will be that you will have to release Butch after each successful exercise, because he'll want to mouth or play with his toy. Without this reinforcement, the toy lure won't work. Gradually, you'll be able to have Butch do more behaviors with fewer playtime releases. It does, however, tend to take a little longer to lure into a behavior with a toy than it does with food.

Finally, we discuss luring with touch. Generally, you won't be able to lure Butch with the promise of touch. There's

LEFT: Put one hand under your dog's chin and the other just in front of his hip bones. RIGHT: As you gently push his chin up, gently press his hips down.

really no means of letting him know that you intend to touch him if he'll sit for you. Instead of luring Butch into position, you'll have to place him there using touch, of course. Once he's in position, pet him in a favorite spot, such as his chest or tummy, or rub his ears. After several repetitions, Butch will pick up on the fact that he'll be petted and will gladly do anything for the touch reward. To pair the use of the clicker with this reward method, you'll probably need three hands. It'll be easiest to use the clicker at a later time, when Butch has a better understanding of the

exercise and you don't have to actually place him into position. When you do use the clicker, you can click/praise the second he attains the sit position and then pet him.

It really won't take too many tries to have a dog that sits on command. Even many of the most assertive personalities will sit for a treat. Once Butch has an idea of how to sit for a treat, you can incorporate the sit into his behavioral repertoire in many ways. He can sit at your side when you are heeling. He can sit for attention versus jumping up for attention. He can sit when you are examining or

bridge and reward. He will also tend to remain closer to your side while heeling, for you are keeping his attention on you even after stopping.

To teach Butch to sit for attention, do the following:

1. When he's jumping up on you, move away. Don't give him any positive attention. Just speaking to him can be a reward to him, so don't say a word.

2. Show Butch the treat. Place it between his eyes.

3. Say "Butch, Sit." Use a commanding tone of voice. Don't yell or repeat.

4. Lure him into position.

5. As soon as he attains this position, click/praise and reward.

Place the target between the dog's eyes. As his head goes up, his rear goes down into a sit.

bathing him. To work the sit into the heeling routine, do the following:

1. Have your dog walk with you for a couple of steps. As you stop, show Butch the treat, hold it just out of his reach between his eyes and say "Butch, Sit" as you stop.

2. When Butch's rump touches down, click/praise and reward.

3. Repeat throughout your heeling exercise. Within a short time, Butch will be sitting automatically when you stop.

You have now paired two behaviors together. Butch now must do more to attain his

You can teach your dog to sit for attention so that he's not apt to seek attention in undesirable ways such as barking and jumping up.

Once the dog sits, click and give him the reward.

6. Repeat as necessary.

In order for this to work, you'll need to be very observant of Butch's behavior. If he just happens to come up to you and sit, you'll need to reward him with much enthusiasm. If you don't, he will return to jumping on you for attention. Teaching Butch to sit while being examined and groomed will require teaching him to stay, and that's covered in the next chapter.

Now we've come to one of the more difficult behaviors to teach: the down. In order to understand why this may be difficult, you first need to realize that lying down is a submissive behavior. Dogs feel very open to attack when in that position and will only assume it on their own if showing subservience to a dominant animal. Telling Butch to lie down on command is counter to his own desires. Many dogs won't do it even for the finest porterhouse steak. Put his head down to retrieve the food? Of course! But place his whole body down? No way!

There are several ways to lure Butch into a down position. You can do it either in front of him or from the heeling position. Your position will have much to do with whether or not Butch is easy to lure downward or obstinate about attaining the position. Here's how to lure into the down position from in front of Butch (for the non-dominating, easy-going dog):

1. Stand in front of Butch and request the sit.

2. As soon as he sits, click/praise and reward.

3. Show him your hand with the treat inside and have him target on it, click/praise and reward.

4. Lower your hand directly

Before guiding into the down position, first show your dog the target.

under his nose. Have Butch target on it. Click/praise and reward as he does so.

5. Gradually lower the target until it touches the ground. As Butch targets, he'll need to lower his shoulders more and more each successive time.

6. Your goal is to have Butch lying down, tummy touching

Dogs have no problem assuming the down position on their own but may not like it as much when commanded to do so.

As the dog targets, give the visual cue (finger pointing downward) and the down command.

the ground. Within a few repetitions, he should do this without your having to touch him. However, as soon as he accomplishes the down behavior, click/praise and reward along with a release from work and a belly rub.

7. The next time you do this exercise, pair the command word with the cue so that Butch can begin learning the meaning of your words while already fully understanding the exercise, making it less like correction and more like a game.

Once Butch has a general understanding of the down command, you can repeat the exercise using the target stick or just a visual cue, always using the bridge and reward at the appropriate time. Once you've been able to establish a behavior threshold, i.e., he will remain in position for a couple of seconds prior to receiving his reward, you'll be able to begin teaching the down/stay.

Here's how to lure the dog into the down from the heel position (used with the obstinate dog):

1. Practice heeling and sitting. Always begin with behaviors that Butch knows well and in which he is receiving positive feedback.

2. After a couple minutes, have Butch sit at your side.

3. With Butch in heel position, put your hand target directly beneath his nose and allow him to sniff the treat.

4. Lower your hand to the ground as you give the down command.

5. If he lowers himself, bravo! He really learns quickly. If not, continue on.

6. Holding your target directly under his nose, put some pressure just behind his shoulder blades. If this is enough for Butch to decide to lower himself, click/praise and reward.

7. If this isn't enough to get your dog into the down position, you'll need both hands to place Butch into position yourself. It'll take four hands to hold a treat or clicker when you do this. Thus you will put the clicker away and apply pressure just behind his shoulder blades with the hand closest to him (left hand if he is on your left side and right hand if he is on your right side).

8. As you apply the pressure, bring his forelegs directly forward as you guide Butch into the down position. As soon as his belly touches the ground, praise verbally and give him his reward. Go directly into the heel exercise. As he accepts being placed into position,

praise and have him remain a second or two longer prior to receiving his reward. This will prepare him for the down/stay.

Butch will go down easier and easier with each successive down exercise. As soon as he does so without your having to place him, you can again pair the click with the verbal praise and reward.

Once your dog has a good understanding of the sit and down commands close to you, it is time to teach these exercises from a distance. You can do this with cues from your target stick, using it as an extension of your hand. Begin by giving the cues with the target stick while Butch is close to you. For sit, raise the target stick straight up.

Lower your target all the way to the floor.

and reward when he touches the stick with his nose.

2. Move the target stick over Butch's head, between his eyes, as you tell him to sit. The end of the stick should be just out of reach. When he looks up, touches the stick with his nose and sits, click/praise and reward.

3. Move a foot away from Butch and repeat the exercise. This time Butch can't really reach the stick, but he does see the movement. As you lift the stick upward, give your dog the sit command. If Butch responds properly, click/praise and reward. If not, bring the stick closer and repeat. Sometimes you need to regress a bit to

ABOVE: Gentle pressure on the shoulder blades helps in getting a reticent dog to fully assume the down position. RIGHT: No matter how near or far you are from the dog, you must be able to keep his attention on you.

This will be a great distance cue, for it will stick out from your silhouette. From a distance, dogs don't see details, they see shapes. Movement really catches their eyes, as do shape differences. The cue for down from a distance should be pointing the stick at the ground at your side. You can use different visual cues; just be consistent and consider a dog's distance-perception abilities.

To teach the sit from a distance:

1. Have Butch target on the end of the stick. Click/praise

maintain the positive response. The lack of understanding may bring frustration to both human and dog. If you frustrate Butch, he'll possibly shut down, no longer interested in progressing. He'll have disdain for the training sessions instead of a desire to work. This is why keeping things positive and rewarding for him is so important, even if it means temporarily slowing your progress.

4. Gradually shape the sit-from-a-distance behavior by increasing the amount of space between you and Butch with each successful exercise. Take your time and do it right. Don't skip too far ahead and always make sure that you make it easy enough for your dog to understand each increment.

Your goal distance depends on you. The goal can be set at 20 feet or 100 feet, or anywhere in between, as long as you are in an enclosed area. With each training session, strive to attain a small increment of that goal.

To teach the down from a distance, you can start the exercise either from a sit/stay, during relaxation time or while performing the recall (the dog's coming when called). The down-from-a-distance exercise can be used for herding, therapy work, obedience or just plain safety. The uses are as varied as your imagination.

A tummy rub is a great reward for lying down!

It's easiest to begin this exercise from a sit/stay, so you might want to read ahead and work on the stay prior to trying this command. Step in front of Butch and signal the down command as you say "Butch, Down." You can signal with your target stick or your finger. Whichever visual cue you decide to use, be consistent throughout. As soon as Butch is in the down position, click/ praise and reward. Repeat the exercise often. However, don't do it more than two or three

ABOVE: Gradually increase your distance from the dog when giving commands. RIGHT: A good distance cue for "Down" is a raised hand.

A good distance cue for "Come" is patting your chest with a raised arm.

times in succession. You wish to teach Butch the cue commands, not pattern-train him. Always mix up the exercises so that Butch stays "on his toes" and so neither of you get bored.

When your dog can perform the down from your face-to-face position, back up a step or two. Do the same visual/verbal cue for down. Again, when he attains the position, click/praise and reward. If he does not go into position, move a step closer and try again. If the closer proximity didn't make a differ-ence, back up to the beginning, standing directly in front of him.

Build on the successes, not the failures. With each incremental success, increase the criteria. First be successful at one step, then at two, and so on until you reach your goal. Always reinforce with praise and rewards whenever working on something new. Eventually, you'll only need to use the praise as a bridge, rewarding when an entire array of exercises has been completed.

The next step is to teach Butch to first target, then sit and lie down. This is a series of behaviors that is called chaining. After each individual behavior has been taught, you can chain them together however you please. Your dog already knows the cues/commands and should perform whichever behavior you request. Chaining truly tests a dog's behavior thresholds. Butch will learn to perform a couple of behaviors with merely a bridge, not receiving his reward until after the complete chain. The more behaviors Butch can do without extinguishing his desire to perform, the higher his behavior threshold. As dogs progress in their training and learn to enjoy the activity for the mere interaction and exercise, the higher their behavior thresholds develop.

Now that Butch can perform a down from a sit at a distance, he needs to learn to do it while moving, something we call the "down-on-the-fly." He'll most likely be moving while playing, herding or running toward you, and during obedience routines. A most important time for him to do a down while moving is if he is starting to come to you from across a street and you see a vehicle coming. You can signal him into a down so that he stays safely put instead of

crossing the street at that time. If you and your dog are doing therapy work, the two of you may encounter someone who is frightened of dogs. Butch can lie down to assume a less frightening appearance, thereby reassuring the startled person.

The best place to begin is while heeling. Every 20 steps or so, give the visual cue/command for the down while moving forward. Always click/praise and reward at the moment that Butch attains that position. If he doesn't go down quickly at first, never fear. It's just a matter of acclimation to the exercise. Butch will discover that the faster he goes down, the sooner he receives his reward. It might help at this point to use a lure to stop him in his tracks and get him to drop down. You can use either your hand as a target or the target stick with food on the end. This will give him an immediate reward that can later be bridged and delayed a bit.

Another segment you'll need to work with is teaching Butch to assume the down position as you place yourself in varying positions—in front, behind and on each side of him. The target stick will help with this, as regardless of where you are standing, the signal remains the same, with the target stick pointed downward. Begin very close so that you can back up your command if Butch either doesn't understand or refuses, so you can guide him into the correct behavior as you praise him. As always, it is important to never give more than one command. If your dog is a regular food hound, he will follow the treat into the down position, especially if he already has an understanding of the exercise. As Butch learns to go down on command with you standing anywhere around him, gradually increase the distance. Remember to work in small increments, using successive approximation as you bridge and reward each step.

If Butch tries to follow the target stick, you might want to place a stationary target at the location in which you will be telling him to lie down. This will allow him to concentrate on remaining in place instead of following you or the ever-moving-into-the-distance target stick. When you've reached the point at which Butch will be moving toward you and you want him to assume the down position as he's on his way in, he will see the target and drop near it. This will need to be phased out, however, because in real life you cannot place a target everywhere you want Butch to drop down! After teaching your dog to perform a stay and recall (discussed later), you can further develop this exercise into a drop-on-recall or down-on-the-fly. You have just a few more behaviors to accomplish prior to this goal.

For training at a distance, place a target where you wish your dog to lie down.

STAY

Regardless of the position, the stay exercise is done using successive approximation shaping. From one second to ten minutes, everything is done in small increments to allow for success. Always strive to let your dog feel successful in everything he does. This will encourage him to continue performing and look forward to working with you. Training should be fun for both of you. When the fun stops, reassess your methods. It might just be that you need to back up a little to regain that success or you need to change your approach. With positive dog training, the most common error is going too fast or not presenting the exercises clearly in the first place.

The stay exercises must be started in very short time increments. Your criteria will be short second-by-second intervals,

Step out on your right foot as you give the hand cue for "Stay."

gradually increasing the number of seconds with each exercise. Don't expect Milo to remain in place for ten seconds on the first couple of rounds. Ten seconds doesn't seem very long…until you start teaching the stay! Some dogs may surprise you and stay for a good amount of time right off the bat, but this isn't the best means of setting up future success. Begin with a mere two seconds and gradually build from there. It might seem too easy, but that's the way it should be. Easy means successful. Success means joy in performance and the desire to continue.

We will begin with the sit/stay. Practice this exercise both while facing Milo and from the heel position. Use the same visual cue and verbal command regardless of where you are standing

Continuous targeting helps maintain a sit/stay.

when you give the command. Begin with Milo in a sit position. Be sure to praise the second he attains the sit. Bring your visual cue in front of his face as you give the stay command. Your visual cue should be something clearly

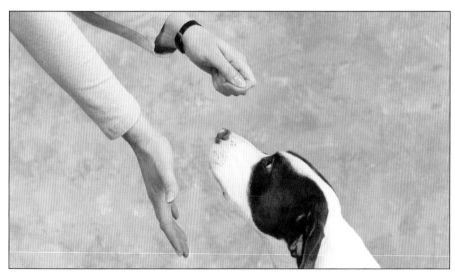

As your dog targets, give the stay command along with the visual cue.

Targeting on a stick while performing the stay.

identifiable, like the palm of your hand with your fingers spread apart. Always precede the command with your dog's name.

If you are facing Milo, remain in front of him. If you are in the heel position, step directly in front of your dog, using the leg other than the one you use when starting into the heel. For example, if you step forward on your left leg first for the heel, then step in front of Milo on your right leg for the stay exercise.

Hold the target near Milo's nose. As he remains in place, nose on target, praise him. After a mere two to three seconds, click/praise and reward, then continue into the heel again or release him from his work. Do something other than trying to make him continue sitting.

Within a few minutes, do the stay exercise again. This time, have Milo hold the position for five seconds prior to bridging and rewarding. Always end the stay by

Targeting on a treat during the stay helps puppies stay focused and learn.

Targeting on a treat helps the dog maintain the sit/stay as you move around him.

Targeting on a stick is also helpful in teaching the dog to maintain the sit/stay as you move around him.

Do this for several training sessions, encouraging your dog through success instead of constant repositioning. Everything should be taught in gradual steps. Rome wasn't built in a day, just as Rin Tin Tin and Lassie weren't saving lives after one training session. It takes time to perfect anything. Take your time and do it right.

Once Milo can maintain the sit/stay for at least 45 seconds, you can begin adding your

going on to something else. Don't allow your dog to get up on his own. If at any time Milo gets up while you are doing the stay exercise, lure him back into position with the target/food and repeat the stay command, complete with visual cue. While working on the initial stays of just a few seconds, Milo is not as likely to break the position, but as you increase the time, he may.

There may be a certain point, say at 30 seconds, where your dog simply can't maintain the position and keeps getting up. If this is the case, back up a bit to 20 seconds.

movement into the criteria. As with anything else, this should be done using successive approximation, gradually adding more and more movement with each stay exercise. Begin by moving side to side while facing Milo. Just one step in each direction. Return to the heel position, click/praise and reward. To encourage your dog to remain in place, praise him the entire time. This way, you are reinforcing through praise, which will maintain his attention on you and reassure him that he is doing what you want.

If this first foray into movement was successful, go to the next stage and move two steps

Once you can move from side to side in front of the dog, go to each side and finally behind him.

Once you are successful at adding your movement into the sit/stay close to the dog, you will gradually increase your distance away from him.

Eventually, you will be able to walk in a complete circle around the dog.

exercise, continue to praise your dog, then return to heel position or move him into another command directly after you click and give him his reward.

Now that you have taught Milo to remain sitting for upwards of a minute while you walk all the way around him, you can begin adding another factor—distance. After all, what good is a stay if you can't walk away? If Milo is reliable with remaining in his sit while you move around, this added criterion of distance shouldn't pose a problem. However, if your dog is at all insecure or has separation issues, trying to gain distance can be tricky. You'll have to proceed a little more slowly, always aware of the particular point at which Milo becomes unstable.

Just as you moved around Milo with ever-increasing increments, so will you increase distance from him with the same method. Begin by doing the sit/stay exercise at the level with which your dog is familiar. Remain close and walk around him in both directions. Try to walk around at least three times before bridging and continuing into another exercise. This will assure you that Milo is ready for the next level of distance work.

On the first try, step away from Milo, just a foot or two away, while you walk around him. Take care to not step straight back and

in each direction. Again, praise throughout, click and reward upon returning to heel position. Once Milo does well with you moving side to side in front of him (still remaining close, mind you), begin moving alongside him on both sides. Gradually increase your movement with each successful stay exercise. If at any time he gets up and you have to replace him into position, go back a few steps and rebuild.

With success in moving along each side of Milo, you can then go on to moving completely around him. Be sure to go in alternating directions so that Milo doesn't become accustomed to only one direction. As you elongate this movement through the stay then proceed to walk around. Stepping back might cause your dog to get up and come toward you, for you have given body language similar to that used in the come command. To avoid this misunderstanding and to make your movement not as obvious, gradually increase the distance as you walk around. Praise the entire time.

When you have done a complete circle at least once, bridge and reward, then go into something else. The next time, increase the distance a few more feet and try for a couple times around. Within five or six sit/stay exercises, you should be able to be six feet away from Milo as you walk around him. After several weeks of consistent practice, you should be able to increase this distance to 30 or 40 feet in your enclosed area.

If your dog is having problems with remaining in place while you move away, use the target stick. Begin by holding it by his nose as you move around, gradually increasing your distance. When you get to the point where you can no longer keep the stick by his nose, lay it on something like a stool, with the end near your dog. Milo may just need something to help him focus, and the target stick should do it. He knows that when he targets, he's sure to get a goodie. Continuously targeting as you move around will teach him

to hold still instead of becoming insecure when you aren't at his side. You will need to bridge and reward more often, however, for without this constant reinforcement, Milo can still feel insecure.

Everything you did for the sit/stay will also apply for the next exercise, the down/stay. Once Milo is lying down, present your visual cue in front of his face, along with his target, as you tell him to stay. Make him remain only a few seconds, then click and reward. Move him out of the down position by either taking him forward into a heel or releasing him from his work. If Milo has any difficulty at all with this position, it would be best to offer as much reward as possible

Sometimes touching your dog as you move around him will be enough to encourage him to remain in a sit/stay.

Once the stay is complete, move into another exercise, like the heel.

when he remains in the down and then release him immediately, offering your touch reward as well. You'll need to make this behavior one of the most positive things Milo could do. This way, he'll learn to ignore his instinct of self-preservation and lie down because it has a very positive outcome.

In the beginning, just remain in heel position with your hand near Milo's shoulder blades. This will enable you to replace him in the down position should he try getting up. If he is constantly trying to get up, you should shorten the length of the down/stay and go back to the point where he remained as long as he was targeting. Sometimes you'll need to do it this way for just a few more days prior to

moving the target away while he remains in place.

Gradually shape Milo's down/stay until he can remain in place for a full minute. This will ensure a solid behavior prior to adding other criteria. If you move too soon, all of the positive punishment necessary to replace Milo into the down position might give your dog a negative feeling about the exercise. You're better off taking your time and doing it right.

When you reach the point where Milo can remain in the down for a minute, you can begin movement around him. The main difference between the sit/stay and the down/stay is that you should begin your movement behind your dog during a down/stay instead of in front of

Shifting the dog's hips to the side aids in a more comfortable, longer-lasting down/stay.

The distance can be gradually increased with each success.

him as in the sit/stay. In order to be assured that Milo will remain in the down/stay, you may want to roll his hips to the side. This position will cause him to take longer to get to his feet, giving you some visual cue that he's about to get up. With more time to lure him back into position, you can preempt his breaking the command, thus making sure he fully understands the meaning of down/stay, when you use your secondary punisher, the word "No," in a low tone of voice.

The first few attempts at movement should be along the dog's side. Go a few steps toward his rear, then back into heel position. Praise him the entire time he remains in position. This reinforces without ending the exercise. When you are ready to end the exercise, click and reward, then continue on to something else. The next time, try to get all the way behind Milo. Praise him the entire time he remains in place, then return to his side, click, give him his reward and move into another behavior.

When Milo can remain in the down/stay with you walking along his side and behind him, try to go

A target stick will help during a down/stay.

In the down/stay, move behind your dog before going in front of him.

Reward your dog as he remains in the down/stay.

Walking around your dog is a great distraction-proofing exercise.

around to his other side. Again, once he has learned to remain in place for this level of criteria, click, reward and then continue on. Within a few down/stay exercises, you should be able to walk completely around Milo and gradually increase your distance from him as you offer your secondary reward, praise, throughout his good response. Your praise will encourage Milo to remain in place, for he knows it's the right thing to do in order to receive the ultimate reward—click and treat (or toy).

If your dog is at all dubious about remaining in the down/stay position, try using the target stick as you did with the sit/stay. A long enough stick will allow you to maintain the target near his nose as you make a complete circle around him.

Now that your dog will perform both sit/stays and down/stays, you can add another part to the down-on-the-fly or drop-on-recall behavior. Place Milo in a sit/stay, then walk in front of him and tell him to do the down/stay. With each subsequent drop (down) exercise, gradually increase your distance from him (and direction) with each successful reaction. Build on this slowly to ensure that the process remains positive. Also, mix it in with practicing other exercises so that it doesn't get old. The more variety, the more attentive your dog will remain.

Within a short time, you should be able to move completely around your dog.

Next, try having your dog do a down/stay while you practice the drop when heeling. Do the down-on-the-fly, then tell him to stay and walk around him. Return to heel position, click and reward, then continue forward into the heel. Don't practice this more than three times in succession before going on to something else. You don't want to create this pattern for every stop. The entire process of the drop-on-recall will come together once you teach Milo to perform a recall (coming when called), which is explained in the next chapter.

For the drop on command, as you heel, tell your dog to go into the down, using your target stick to lure him into position.

A dog who comes when called can be given more freedom to run in safe areas.

RECALL AND DISTRACTION-PROOFING

A RELIABLE RECALL

Teaching your dog to come to you when you call him (known as the recall) is one of the most important lessons in your dog's existence. With reliability in this behavior, Rover gains freedom and you gain confidence in your beloved dog. You can go to the park and allow your dog to run and play. You can take him to the beach and let him swim. You can go hiking and allow him to romp

Even young puppies can learn to come reliably when called.

Leaning forward as you step backward invites your dog to come to you.

beside you in the woods. The possibilities are endless. The main benefit, however, is the safety of your dog.

Rover will need to come to you regardless of what he is doing, no matter where you are calling him from and despite the distractions in his vicinity. In order to accomplish this goal, you'll need to break it down into much smaller pieces. The first segment is to perform a recall from a short distance, in an area where there are no distractions. Make certain that Rover is on a leash so that you can back up your command (show him the correct response) if something distracts him. Very

likely you will not have to apply any positive punishment if you use a lure along with inviting body language and a happy vocal tone (the latter two which you must always use whenever you call your dog). The lure can be food or a toy, or simply your low positioning (crouched down) and your welcoming voice. Be sure to practice from any stay position as well as during Rover's break time when he's not working. Varying the conditions will reinforce future responses.

The next breakdown will be distance. Begin with a mere two feet. This will ensure success. Begin by showing your target to Rover. Bridge and reward when he touches it with his nose. Pull the target closer to yourself as you bend at the waist or crouch down to his level. Speak in soothing "come hither" tones, giving the command "Come." Rover will learn this quickly, for it is all very attractive to him. As Rover responds, praise. When he arrives at your feet, click and reward.

The next time, increase your distance to four feet away. With that success, progress to six feet. Gradually increase the distance with each success. Make certain the recall is solid and reliable from all positions at a given distance before moving on to a greater distance. Rover should

When your dog
looks at you, click.

come to you regardless of the direction from which you are calling him. Make Rover's arrival as pleasant as possible so that he always knows that coming to you is the best thing he can do.

If you are practicing on leash, as you should when you begin any new exercise, take precautions to not put any pressure on the leash as you move around your dog. The slightest pressure can urge Rover out of his stay before you wish him to move. It will take some time and conditioning to teach your dog not to move when the leash is being tugged. He's not there yet, so be careful.

Practicing the recall off-leash will be tricky, as you have no means of backing up your command or keeping Rover from becoming more enthusiastic about another activity. Only pursue the off-leash recall if you are in a small enclosed environment where you can quickly regain Rover's attention.

As your dog learns to come from longer and longer distances, switch over to a longer leash of lighter weight. I would suggest something made of cotton that is 20 feet long. Cotton is easy to hold and easy to clean, and, believe me, you will need to clean it often, for it will be dragging along in the dirt, mud and whatever else is on the ground. However, don't make the leash longer than you can handle. It takes practice to gather a long leash. I have found that reeling the leash in like a hose, outdoor extension cord or boat rope works best. In this manner, you can quickly gather it without incurring knots and throwing it around as your dog comes to you. Should Rover see you playing with the leash, he's sure to want to join in the fun.

I suggest you hold your clicker in your right hand, along with the end of the leash. If your clicker is attached to a coiled wrist band or retractor, that's even better. Use your left hand to slide the leash through, stop when there is approximately two to three feet of leash between your hands, slip it into your right hand and slide through again. With this motion, the entire leash can be gathered within three or four grabs. No knots. No confusion. Also, you'll be able to bridge your dog upon his arrival in front of you in a timely fashion.

WORKING WITH DISTRACTIONS

Once Rover can do the recall reliably both indoors and outdoors in a quiet, closed-in space, start adding some minor distractions. Leave a few of his toys lying about. Enlist the help of a friend or family member

LEFT: Stretch the leash between your arms. RIGHT: Bring the leash together in one hand; repeat. BELOW: Continue to gather until you have the entire leash looped in one hand.

and ask the person to walk around, clap his hands, slap his legs, make noise and, finally, throw the toys about. Each distraction has to be introduced in a graduated manner. For example, Rover must first learn to listen with his toys present. When he understands to pay attention to you instead of the toys, you can add a person. The next step is to have the person moving. Follow with the person walking around, whistling or clapping. Next, have the person jog around. Then ask the person to pick up and drop the toys. With that accomplished, the person begins throwing the toys

Toys present a great distraction during the recall exercise.

about, first far from Rover, then closer and closer as Rover ignores the toys and, instead, watches you. With the toy distractions accomplished, it's time to make it really tough: working in the presence of other dogs. This can often be the most difficult distraction (besides maybe a cat, squirrel or rabbit). The second dog should already be well versed in canine/canine distraction-proofing. If not, things will be far more difficult, for both dogs will be vying to play with each other.

Begin the other-dog distraction at a distance, far enough away so that Rover takes little notice. Gradually work the dog closer and closer. When Rover begins to look at the other dog, keep the distraction dog at that point, no closer. In order to maintain your dog's attention, you'll need to shape his response to you. When he looks at you, click and reward. When he looks away from you, do something that will regain his attention.

It is often the case that when confronted with a very desirable distraction, such as another dog, no amount of treats, promise thereof, toys or coaxing will work to regain your dog's attention. Even negative punishers won't work. (Your dog won't care if you ignore him or take away his reward.) The only thing that might work in

effectively without causing physical or mental harm to your dog.

Once you have each particular distance conquered, gradually decrease the distance incrementally. When Rover looks at you, click and reward. When he looks away, apply the positive punishment. You should also be using your voice as secondary reinforcement and punishment. When Rover looks at you, praise him. When he looks away, use a low tone with your correction word. Eventually, all you will need is your

A food lure might maintain your dog's attention while working around distractions.

this situation is a positive punisher, such as using a head halter to apply pressure on his nose, or a neck collar to deliver a quick reminder that he's to maintain his attention on you. The tool you use depends on your skill and on your dog. While most dogs can be taught to pay attention regardless of distraction with a head halter, there are many who will never adjust to wearing one. At this point, consult with a professional dog trainer, who should know what tool to use and can teach you how to apply it

As the dog becomes reliable, praise alone will maintain his attentiveness.

voice, but initially you will need to reinforce with the appropriately timed and applied bridge, reward and positive punishment.

Before you progress to working Rover on the long leash, make certain that he can perform with all of the different distractions on his six-foot lead. You don't need to be struggling with a handful of leash while trying to distraction-proof your dog. It is important to note that distraction-proofing can be shaped into place with any and all commands, not just the recall. First, Rover must fully understand each exercise. Then, gradually add the distractions as discussed. In time, Rover will perform everything you request, regardless of what is going on around him. This all takes time, patience and loads of repetition. Practice. Practice. Practice!

DROP ON RECALL
Now that all the pieces are in place, we can fully put together the drop-on-recall exercise. Just a reminder: always backtrack and practice the behaviors and exercises in which you and Rover are comfortable and successful prior to starting anything new. This begins each training session on a positive note, with your dog receiving lots of praise and rewards. There are two exercises you'll be expanding: the down-on-the-fly and the distance drop.

First, the down-on-the-fly. After you have Rover drop

In the drop on recall, give your dog the verbal and visual cues for the down command just before he arrives to you.

Begin the come from the down/stay at only a short distance from the dog.

away. Move around him as you gain some distance. Have Rover do a recall. Praise him as he comes to you. Just before his arrival, give the signal and command for the down. If he goes directly into the down position, click/praise and reward. If not, step in toward him and help him attain the position through luring and/or placing, always praising when he is in position. If you had to help Rover into the down, you should return to practicing the down from a distance.

down while you are walking, tell him to perform a stay. Leave his side and walk around. Stop somewhere around him and have him do a recall. This establishes his coming to you from a down position regardless of what he did prior to the down.

Second, the come from the down/stay. Have Rover do a sit/stay, walk a short distance away and signal for a down/stay. Walk away a little farther and have him perform a recall.

Great. Now we're set. Let's shape this drop-on-recall! Put Rover in a sit/stay or down/stay. Praise, but no click yet! Walk

Once Rover can perform this drop from a mere foot or two in front of you on his way in, try to gain a bit of distance by telling him to perform the down sooner, as he is farther away from you. With each correct response, click/praise and reward.

You can also use your target stick to help Rover understand where to go down. The touch exercise can be very helpful. Place Rover in a sit/stay. Walk away and praise as he remains in the sit/stay. Place the target stick or Alley Oop where you wish your dog to drop down.

Instruct him to touch, and then click/praise and reward when he reaches the target. Then have him do a down/stay. Walk away and praise as he remains in the down/stay position. Call him to come, click/praise and reward.

Build on this by gradually being farther and farther away from the target stick as Rover gets up, goes to the stick, touches and then goes down, followed by the recall, where he receives his bridge and reward. If there are any misunderstandings along the way, back up a step or two and break the exercise down into even smaller goals. Rushing Rover may incur confusion, which will cause him to no longer enjoy himself. Your dog must love what he's doing in order to learn with enthusiasm and look forward to future training sessions. Keep it simple. Keep it short. Keep it positive!

With your dog in a sit/stay, walk away and place the target stick where you want him to drop down on his way in to you.

POSITIVE REINFORCEMENT IN EVERYDAY LIFE

Positive-reinforcement training is extremely helpful in allowing you to reshape your dog's behavior to eliminate bad behavior and bring on good behavior. Just about every puppy and new dog will go through stages of trying to obtain something rewarding by demanding attention in an annoying fashion. Unfortunately, the things he might try can be destructive in some form or another, dangerous for him and you or just purely annoying.

Crate-training helps with house manners, safety and clean potty habits.

Here's how it goes: Rascal will try something new. If he finds some reward in it, he will continue the behavior. Should he find no reward, the behavior will become extinct. The end result is up to you. You can shape his behavior by rewarding what you want, or you can give him no reward or even a punishment when he does something you don't want. The positive-punishment factor should only be employed if he is being stubborn about a specific behavior and no amount of negative punishment has worked. You can only ignore his chewing your shoes and stealing food from the kitchen counter for so long! In this chapter, we discuss some common issues with which dog owners can be faced and how to handle these issues.

HOUSE-TRAINING

There's an easy way and a hard way to house-train, or housebreak, your puppy or dog (don't assume that an adopted adult dog is already housebroken!). If you want to go with the easy way, be watchful and consistent. Otherwise, you're heading for the hard way, which means punishment, a bad attitude and inevitable frustration.

Your diligence in house-training will be well worth it. Your dog will learn faster and you will set a stronger pattern for future behavior. It will also keep Rascal in a positive frame of mind with less chance of developing a "guilty conscience." By this, I mean his crouching in fear anytime you walk into the room. Yes, dogs have very good memories. If parameters have been set and your dog usually adheres to them, he will remember if he "screws up." Many dogs will try to avoid the area in which the blunder took place. This can be perceived as a guilty conscience.

You can easily apply your shaping work to teaching a pup where to potty. It's as easy as taking him to the desired location, saying the potty cue word over and over and, when he does his business, click/praise and reward. It's best to do this when you're certain of success, such as first thing in the morning after he's "held it" through the night (in his crate, of course). Ah, but I'm jumping ahead. There are smaller steps that you might need to take prior to this. Let's first break crate-training down piece by piece.

Crate training. No, it's not a cruel thing. In fact, it's very humane. The crate simulates a safe den where Rascal feels the sides all around him. Nothing is scarier to a

dog than to be in confinement without feeling the sides of his den. Most destructive behaviors occur under these conditions, such as his being locked in a room, locked in a small outdoor pen or tied up. The dog is confined, but he doesn't feel safe. In a crate, Rascal feels safe. Nothing can attack him behind his back because he feels solidity there. He can see what's coming. This is a natural instinctual response.

So on to crate training. If Rascal doesn't go into the crate on his own, you'll need to teach him to go in on command. Keep in mind that this is Rascal's safe place, not a place of punishment. Never put Rascal into his crate to punish him; always make him feel that the crate is a happy place. Begin with the crate door wide open. Sit on the floor near it and place treats at the opening. When Rascal goes for the treats, click and praise. Do this each time he goes for a treat.

Now put the treat just inside the opening. When he goes for the treat,

Initially, your puppy should be allowed to come out of the crate whenever he wishes as long as you're there to supervise.

Dogs feel secure in their crates, their own personal "dens."

click and praise. Gradually place the treat farther and farther inside the crate. Always click and praise as he gets his treat. Within a short period of time, Rascal will be thinking of the crate as a treat-dispensing machine, a fantastic place!

Now add a command for this behavior, such as "Kennel up." This should be said in an enthusiastic tone of voice, equivalent to inviting Rascal into a game. After all, he will be going into the treat dispenser, so it will be a great thing! As soon as Rascal walks in, click and praise and throw in a treat. Repeat this a few times until Rascal learns that he may not receive the treat as soon as he enters, but rather a few seconds later, after entering and turning around to face you. That's the beauty of the bridging. He knows the treat is on its way and no longer needs to be baited into the behavior.

Once your dog is comfortable entering the crate on his own, it's time to add the closing of the crate door. Close the door for a brief period, say five seconds. Click/praise, open the door and give Rascal a treat. Next time, add another five seconds. Repeat the exercise, adding five-second increments each time. If Rascal begins to get "antsy," try clicking and praising while he's inside and dropping him a treat. This way, he knows that remaining calm while in the crate also delivers rewards.

The next step is to walk away. Use successive approximation similar to that used for the stay exercises. Begin with standing up. If Rascal remains calm, click/praise and reward. Next, walk side to side in front of the crate. Again, if Rascal remains calm, click/praise and reward. If not, return to the previous step and work on that for a little longer. Gradually increase your movement and distance with each successful exercise. Don't do too much at once or Rascal will become anxious. You want this to be a pleasant experience, not one he'll want to avoid.

With Rascal's acceptance of your not being next to the crate, you'll need to teach him to remain calm and relaxed when you leave the room. Begin with leaving for a couple of seconds. Return, click/praise and put a treat in his crate. You can also let him out for a few minutes and rework the

"Kennel up" exercise a few times. It's always good to mix in the easy stuff with the newer things to maintain a positive attitude.

Gradually increase your time out of the room, always returning and giving Rascal his bridge, praise and reward. Each time you practice crate training, increase the amount of time that you are out of the room. Within a few days, Rascal will feel safe in his den and he can remain there while you take care of errands away from home. The crate will also be his nighttime sleeping location, where he'll learn to control his bowels and bladder until he is let outside. Few dogs will soil their dens. This is another instinctive behavior. The only time this isn't so is with dogs that are never allowed to leave their crates to relieve themselves. They have learned to "go" in their pens. This can also be true of a dog that has been kenneled for a while. He has learned to relieve himself on the concrete floor of his run, for there's nowhere else to go. The concrete of a run closely simulates the surface of some indoor areas, especially unfinished concrete basements, so the dog might think that these indoor areas are fine to use as his bathroom as well.

Moving on with housebreaking, now that we've shaped the crate behavior, it's time to shape Rascal's "going outside" behavior. When you go to take Rascal outdoors, you'll need to teach him how to "tell" you

Reward your dog when he is relaxing quietly in his crate.

that he needs to go. Some of us can naturally read our dogs' messages when they come to us prancing, barking or just putting their heads in our laps. Other owners need to have alarms go off in their ears! Here's a happy medium: teach Rascal to ring a bell at the door. Make sure that the bell will be loud enough for you to hear it wherever you might be. Hang the bell low enough so that Rascal can comfortably reach it with his nose or paw.

Praise your dog as he remains in his crate with the door closed.

You can teach your dog to ring a bell to let you know that he has to relieve himself.

Here's how to do it: upon approaching the door on your way out for a potty trip with Rascal, put a treat on the bell. Make sure it's stuck on well enough that your dog must make the bell move as he licks it off. Generally, a piece of cheese works well for this exercise. Click and praise Rascal as he gets his treat on the bell. As soon as the bell makes noise, take Rascal outdoors and to his relief area. Keep him there and say his potty word over and over until he does his business. Click, praise and give him his treat when he finishes. Do this every time you go outdoors with Rascal. If you are working on teaching him to go potty in a litter box, which some owners of smaller dogs prefer, then use the same theme with the added variation of putting him into his box and not allowing him out until he does his business.

Within a week or so, Rascal will have the idea to ring the bell and potty outdoors (or in his box). This doesn't mean that he's completely house-trained, especially if he is under six months of age or in any way new to your household. You must maintain diligence and observe him at all times. If you can't watch Rascal, he'll need to be somewhere where he can't have an accident, such as in his crate or outside in a fenced-in area.

Should you catch Rascal going to his bell, click/praise and reward. This will reinforce the behavior, making it stronger. Keeping an eye on Rascal will prevent accidents and prevent your having to apply positive punishment to correct his misdeed. If accidents happen, you must apply a positive punishment if you catch him in the act, or Rascal will think that he can do his business in your home. His reward was bladder or intestinal relief.

The hard way to train Rascal would be allowing him access to areas where you can't observe him. Not keeping a potty schedule is another *faux pas*. Not showing him where to go will further degenerate the behavior. It takes time and effort to accomplish house-training; never believe otherwise! Not adhering to the steps I've outlined will result in your having to punish Rascal for something he doesn't fully understand, and that's not fair to human or canine.

JUMPING UP

Jumping up would not be an issue if you had never reinforced the behavior in any manner. However, it's always so cute when Rascal is a pup…he jumps up to say hi and you can't help but pet and hug him. However, when he grows up, whether he's 20 pounds, 50 pounds or 150 pounds, and has muddy feet, it's no longer cute, especially when he greets your elderly aunt with such exuberance. Rascal doesn't know that this is improper. He has received attention of some sort for jumping up in the past, so it's always been rewarding.

What you need to do from the outset is make this behavior extinct. To do so, never give Rascal attention (positive or negative) of any sort when he jumps up. This means no touching, no speaking. These are positive responses. No pushing off or yelling. These are negative responses. Even the negative responses are rewarding to an attention-seeking dog. Redirection is another key to extinguishing this behavior. You need to get Rascal's attention onto something positive, such as sitting for attention. This needs to be done immediately when Rascal tries to jump up, and fully rewarded when accomplished.

To avoid rewarding Rascal for jumping up, turn away and/or step back. Continue to do so as long as he jumps. If this doesn't work, you'll need to apply some sort of negative reinforcer, such as a noise box or squirting him in the face with water. A noise box can easily be made out of a small metal can with 15 pennies inside. When Rascal jumps up, shake the can in an up-and-down motion once or twice. The noise will startle him and he'll stop jumping. If your dog is ultra-sensitive to noises, don't use this method. Instead, try filling a spray bottle or squirt gun with water and spritz him in the face as he jumps. Both of these methods are considered positive punishment, as you are adding something to create the punishment. A negative punishment is your turning away. You are taking away his landing zone—you.

The next step or, rather, concurrent step, is redirection. Show Rascal what you want him to do to obtain attention and reward him the second he does so. Most of us

Any form of touch is a reward for the dog's jumping up.

would prefer our dogs to sit when they want attention instead of incessantly jumping on us. Once you have stopped him from jumping, tell Rascal to sit. The second his rear end touches the floor, click/praise and pet him. Each time he comes to sit near you, reward him with petting and praise. You don't have to have a clicker to reinforce this behavior. In this case,

touch is enough reward to promote the appropriate behavior routine. Just be certain that you're aware of Rascal's new attention-seeking pattern (coming to sit) and that you reward him for it, or he'll go right back to jumping up on you because that's a sure means of getting some type of reaction out of you.

THE GARBAGE CAN (AND OTHER OFF-LIMIT OBJECTS)

A dog's getting into the garbage is a tough thing to cure. The food reward alone is enough to promote the behavior. You can't possibly mask the smells coming from the garbage can, nor is there any means of keeping him entirely out of it unless you put it somewhere inaccessible. While making the garbage inaccessible can be arranged, it will not overcome the predilection for garbage-hunting. Dogs can't easily ignore tantalizing scents. The result of their inappropriate actions will have to be unappealing enough to discontinue the practice. Usually it's tough to come up with something more attractive than steak bones and leftover meat loaf. The best tactic is to teach Rascal to not even get near the garbage can. It's as off-limits as, say, your Ming vase or Italian leather shoes. Regardless of the object, Rascal can learn to keep his mouth and paws away.

To condition your dog to leave your valuables (this includes your trash cans) alone, you'll need to

The dog will not find jumping up as fun when he is ignored.

apply some type of aversive when he nears or shows interest in these objects. The aversive can be a squirt of water or a startling sound. Then, guide him into a more positive action by using one of his toys to gain his attention and reward him with praise when he redirects his focus to his toy. Again, using a combination of these things (an aversive and then a toy) will be most productive, for the aversive will give Rascal a bad "vibe" from the off-limits object and then he will get a good "vibe" when he avoids the object and goes for a toy.

You will need to remain watchful and diligent to catch your dog in the act of showing interest in the garbage. This can be as subtle as sniffing the air near the garbage can or having his nose on the ground, gradually tracking his way in that direction. Catch him in the act of thinking about that enticing smell and cure it before it occurs, thereby making the entire process clear to him. Communication is the key to reliability, as are consistency and praise.

MOUTHING

Mouthing behavior is often seen in young puppies and in dogs with dominating personalities. Puppies mouth when they play. Dominant dogs mouth to make a point, that point being that they are in charge. You should never, at any time, allow Rascal to mouth you. There's no such thing as soft mouthing

while playing a game. Someone can still be injured and Rascal will pick up the wrong idea of his place in the family pack. You can usually redirect Rascal when he gets into mouthing moods by showing him a toy and moving it around. Dogs go after movement; thus the moving toy becomes more interesting than your stationary arm or foot, unless, of course, you are moving that appendage around as you try to dislodge his teeth, in which case the game just got more interesting.

Another thing you can do is startle him by saying "Ow!" in a high, yipping tone of voice. When dogs play together, they tend to get rough. The "shut-off valve" is either a submissive position or a high-pitched tone from one of the dogs, expressing distress. Few of us will throw ourselves on the floor with our tummies up and heads back, so a yip is the next best thing. As soon as your dog lets go, redirect him to one of his toys and play with him. The entire reason that he's mouthing you is to get you into the game. Play

Rummaging in the garbage is a self-rewarding behavior for a dog, as he's able to explore all of those interesting scents and more than likely find himself something to eat.

the game according to your rules and you can better control Rascal's behavior. Eventually, you'll be in charge of initiating the game.

CHEWING

Most puppies will chew anything and everything. They are testing palatability as well as learning about their environments. It will be up to you to guide Rascal in the right direction. Make sure that your dog has a wide variety of chew toys appropriate to his breed and size. For example, you don't want to offer a squeaky latex toy to a large-breed dog, as the toy will immediately be destroyed and might even be eaten, causing digestive disorders or possibly internal injury. Edible chews should be tested in small quantities to be certain they also don't cause gastric distress.

A good variety of toys will most likely include those made of hard rubber and sturdy nylon in various shapes and flavors, and a sterilized thick shank bone. The shank bone as well as certain rubber toys can be filled with edible substances (like peanut butter), thus keeping Rascal occupied for long periods of time. There are other types of interactive toys, such as "treat cubes" that you can fill with small dog treats; as Rascal plays, a treat will pop out of one of the holes in the toy from time to time. These also keep dogs engaged for long time periods, as they never know when the toy will produce a treat. Dental chews are constructed with small raised knobs or nodes that scrape away plaque as the dog chews. Some dogs love stuffed toys. Others adore toys that make sounds. When you give Rascal these latter two types, be sure he doesn't tear them apart, as the insides and any small pieces (eyes, noses, etc.) can be dangerous if ingested. Actually, it's rather inevitable that Rascal will tear apart soft and squeaky toys, so it's best to offer them only under supervision and remove them at the first sign of being chewed apart.

In order to maintain Rascal's interest in his toys, you'll need to rotate them so that he thinks he's constantly getting new toys. The "newer" toys maintain his interest for longer periods of time. Should Rascal be in the process of teething, offer frozen toys like ice cubes or a washcloth that you've dampened, twisted and frozen. The cold toys

A soft toy will be welcomed by a puppy.

will give his gums relief, reducing teething stress.

With plenty of toys around, you can easily redirect Rascal from chewing the table leg to playing with one of his toys. This will require your constant observation of his activities, which will pay off in the end, for he will learn that your furniture isn't part of his toy box. Plus, he will learn this in a positive manner.

You can take encouraging Rascal to play with his toys a step further by using your bridging device. When Rascal touches one of his toys, click/praise and reward him by playing with him with his toy. You don't always have to reward with food. A toy can be equally satisfying.

EXCESSIVE BARKING

Barking is another self-rewarding behavior, so it will take something either far more attractive or very aversive to stop a dog from excessive barking. Your yelling at Rascal to be quiet just adds to the fun, as you have joined in the "barkfest" as well! While there are some dogs that can be repro-grammed out of this annoying behavior through positive-reinforcement shaping techniques, there are others that get so much joy out of barking that they won't care what treats, toys or activities you use as bait. Then there are those that will be quiet while you are around but sound off when you're not home. These are more likely territorial barkers. These dogs feel it is their duty to keep strangers at bay, even if they might be squirrels or sparrows. An intruder is a trespasser no matter the size or species.

Some dogs bark due to separa-tion anxiety. You can be relatively sure that your dog has this disorder if he's quiet and relaxed when you're at home, but you get reports from your neighbors that he's spent the day barking at nothing when he's home alone. This type of barking is probably the most difficult to cure. The more the dog is punished for the behavior, the worse it becomes.

It may take some time to cure the excessive barker. To do so using positive reinforcement, you'll need to be consistent and dedicated. It's probably best to use Rascal's meal kibble, otherwise you'll fill him up with treats and he won't want to eat his normal meals. Before you begin,

A dog's barking should not be rewarded with attention, or else you will be encouraging him to bark for attention. Don't even make eye contact.

arm yourself with a pouch or bag to carry his food, a squeaker and the clicker. The squeaker will act as a distracter. The clicker will reinforce and the kibble will reward the appropriate behavior.

To begin, put Rascal in a situation where he would normally bark. While he's quiet, click/praise and reward. If he barks, squeak the squeaker until he stops to investigate. When he does so, click/praise and reward. Repeat throughout the training session. Each time you put Rascal into this situation, be armed with your tools. Use them consistently and be patient. It will take much time to overcome a self-rewarding behavior.

The most difficult part will be conditioning Rascal when you aren't at home. In order to continue using positive-reinforcement techniques, you can't allow Rascal to be in the "barking situation" when you can't reinforce his reactions. To do this will undo all that you've accomplished. If you have no choice but to put Rascal "into the fire" (meaning the situation in which he barks), you'll have to use a negative-reinforcement technique. Remember my mentioning that I don't like to resort to these? Well, in this situation it might be necessary.

Negative reinforcement to cure excessive barking generally means a "no bark" collar. There are several types, and the type that you use will depend on your dog. Again, it's best to consult with a professional when you must use an unfamiliar technique. Negative reinforcement will extinguish a behavior using either a painful or uncomfortable sensation. To do so incorrectly could injure Rascal emotionally and/or physically. The different collar types are the citronella collar and the electronic-stimulation collar. The citronella collar will spritz citronella over Rascal's nose each time he barks. If he is sensitive to this, his barking behavior will shortly be extinguished. If not, you'll have to use something that he'll feel, such as the electronic stimulation collar. There are several types of these collars: a type that merely makes a buzzing sound when the dog barks, a type that will immediately shock the dog upon barking and a type that will allow the dog to bark three or four times and then shock him. Generally the shock-type collars have several settings so that you can adjust them according to Rascal's sensitivity.

This is the only time I'll discuss negative reinforcement, as an excessive barking problem can often lead to dire consequences. I've seen excessive barkers end up in shelters, euthanized or operated upon to have their voice boxes removed. All of these extreme measures can be prevented through the dog owner's diligence and care. One must be open-minded and use whatever humane means necessary to ensure that his dog remains a well-loved, well-cared-for family member and not abandoned due to what is a curable behavior.

STEALING

This is similar to the chewing routine: Rascal steals a sock or shoe and commences to rearrange its molecular structure, having a great time while doing so. Often, stealing is a means of obtaining attention. Rascal has learned that if he takes something he's not supposed to have and runs with it, he will launch a great game of tag. There are several ways to handle this. One is to always reward Rascal when he's playing with his toys by joining in on his game. You also have to ignore him when he steals something, such as your laundry, and runs away with it. Usually Rascal does not steal items to end up chewing on

them, but to start the racing-around mayhem that follows such behavior. However, if Rascal is one of those dogs that tend to destroy the spoils of larceny, you will have to get the object back from him rather quickly. Redirection won't work, because the stolen property is reward enough to cause the behavior.

Instead, keep a leash on Rascal. Don't allow him access to anywhere

TOP: Engaging the dog in interactive games with his toys encourages him to choose the correct playthings. BOTTOM: Attention and petting rewards his appropriate behavior.

that you cannot observe him. When he sniffs at or lunges for something he isn't supposed to have, grab the leash and tell him to come. Reward him with praise and try to interest him in a game with one of his toys. Better yet, give him an interactive toy that will occupy his time, such as a treat-filled cube or a hollow shank bone or rubber toy that's been filled with some type of goodie. In this manner, you can redirect Rascal in a positive way, showing him that playing with his own toys is far more rewarding than going after something else.

RUSHING THE DOOR

A dog might rush the door for territorial reasons or to give an exuberant greeting. The method you use to cure the problem greatly depends on the reason for the behavior. Be sure to observe Rascal's overall behavior patterns to discern

A happy dog will smile, pant and hold his ears to the side.

why he's rushing the door. A territorial dog will be snarling, barking, jumping up and possibly scratching at the door. Furthermore, a territorial dog will show dominant body language, such as ears straining forward, tail stiff, hackles raised, body stiff. On the other hand, an exuberant greeter will be barking, jumping up, wagging his tail and running around near the door, wiggling all over, ears down and/or back, bouncing around with delight.

Another door-rushing scenario occurs with the escape artist. You know the type. The grass is always greener with the dog down the block. An escape artist lies in waiting for his chance. The doorbell rings, you open it and whoosh! Out rushes Rascal, initiating a run through the neighborhood that will leave you strained and exhausted, with Rascal coming back in his own sweet time after a romp with the dogs down the street, a snack on the animal carcass he found in the woods and a bath in muddy puddle water, only to shake with satisfaction once he comes inside, covering you in stinky mud as you tremble with fury, trying very hard not to be mean to him because he did make the correct choice to come home, no matter how long it took him to do so.

The best means of addressing these personalities is to form a positive pattern. Begin with always having Rascal stop and sit/stay and/or down/stay at the door. He's not to cross the threshold without your first telling him to heel. Condition him through repetition. Vary the length of the stays and the commands given afterward. For example, on one occasion you pass through the doorway with a heel command. On another occasion you have Rascal perform a recall back into the house. He has to understand that an open door doesn't always mean that he's going out. As your dog accomplishes the short stays, aim for longer ones. Also practice walking around him, hiding behind the door or hiding around the outside wall. Distraction-proof by having other people or another dog walk through.

During the training process, it would be a good idea to always keep a four- to six-foot leash on Rascal while he's inside. This will allow you to stop his escape by either grabbing or stepping on the leash as he's on his way out the door. Then you can give him his sit/stay or down/stay commands and have the means of making certain he follows through. If you happen to have your clicker and treat with you, then use them. If not, as is often the case, just praise and pet him in one of his favorite places. Always show him how much more rewarding it is to remain inside instead of racing through the door. If Rascal is escaping with the sole purpose of socializing, then you might want to consider a second dog. If the grass is greener at home,

he'll tend to remain there.

The stay-at-the-door exercise will also help the exuberant greeter. It teaches him that no one will reward him with touch if he doesn't first control himself. You will need to instruct all those entering your home that they aren't to touch Rascal until he settles down so that he isn't rewarded in any fashion for jumping around. After Rascal remains in his stay for at least one minute, you can release him and pet him, provided he remains sitting. As soon as he pops up, the petting stops.

The cure for a territorial dog is a little more difficult. There is much you'll need to do to redirect his behavior while not extinguishing his effectiveness as a watchdog. First you'll need to establish a "quiet" command, such as "Enough," "Quiet," "Shush," etc. This will need to be rewarded profusely when it is performed, even if it takes a few minutes for the

**"Who's there?"
Some dogs just
can't wait to be
the "welcome
wagon" when you
come home or
when guests come
to your house.**

dog to do so. Second, you'll need a means of redirecting and reinforcing. Redirecting can be done with a bell or rattle. Once Rascal is distracted from his barking and starts to investigate the source of that ring/rattle, click and reward. If Rascal doesn't care about the ring/rattle, you'll have to back up your quiet command by taking hold of his leash and making him perform a down/stay. It would be far better to have him do a down/stay than a sit, for the down is a more submissive position and it is more difficult for him to get up from the down. However, if you haven't the means of backing up your quiet command, i.e., no collar and leash, you'll need to apply positive

punishment. This can be a squirt of water or citronella, a shake of the noise box or taking hold of your dog and pushing down on his nose as you stare into his eyes and apply a secondary verbal punishment—the low-toned word "No." It would be a good idea to utilize a head halter at this time. Sometimes it's easier to apply pressure on Rascal's nose with a leash than trying to get him to hold still enough to grab his muzzle. Swiftness will aid your cause.

Practice having your dog come to you every time he hears a knock on the door or the doorbell. You'll want to teach him how to direct himself at these cues. Repetition will condition. Once you have Rascal's attention, always reinforce this by rewarding him. He has to learn that it is far more positive to pay attention to you and restrain himself than to ignore you and carry on with behavioral outbursts. You have to make the grass greenest on your side of the fence.

COUNTER-SURFING
Yes, yet another self-rewarding behavior. It's going to be tough to convince Rascal that he mustn't "surf" the countertops, meaning jump up and put his front paws on the countertop to investigate, steal or eat whatever he may find there. Counter-surfing has always yielded a reward of some sort. The best place to begin is to keep your counters clear of edibles and things

that might be fun for Rascal to play with. In essence, clear the counters! With nothing to cause temptation, there'll be no reason for the activity.

You can only correct a counter-surfing problem if you are there to see it happen. Therefore, don't give Rascal access to the kitchen or washrooms when you can't watch him. Keep him on his leash at all times so that you can quickly correct his behavior if redirection or an aversive noise doesn't do the job. He shouldn't be allowed to remain on the counter or table as you continually try to redirect or tempt him with a goodie. This alone can be enough to encourage the behavior, as it has grabbed your attention.

Often the noise box will be enough to discourage the behavior. Give a shake of the can with a low-toned verbal reprimand. With consistency and persistence, this alone should extinguish the behavior. A scat mat can also do the trick. I've mentioned that this device emits an electrical pulse that causes discomfort to the animal when he touches it. This is a strong enough aversive to stop the counter-surfers. The scat mat is a negative reinforcer and is something that your dog will want to avoid. Note: this works for cats, too.

You can also employ a trick similar to the one used to stop the dog from rushing the door. If Rascal looks interested in the countertops, redirect him with a squeaker. When he looks at you instead of putting his front paws on the counter, click/praise and reward. With nothing to reward him on the counter, he'll soon learn that all rewards come from you, which will make him follow you around instead of searching the counters for gratification. It's better to have a shadow than a shadowy character!

"Does that taste as good as it smells?" To a counter-surfer, there's only one way to find out! Prevent surfing by removing temptation.

MORE SOURCES OF INFORMATION

In the last ten years, positive-reinforcement training has taken the world by storm. Trainers everywhere are crossing over from traditional methods to using operant conditioning and positive reinforcement, which time and again prove to be effective, humane and fun. From the pioneers of operant conditioning and its thousands of practitioners to those new to animal training, everyone can benefit from the myriad of information available about the methodology, usage and practice of positive reinforcement. Following are some books, videos and websites that will help you learn more about this type of training and how it can be utilized in everyday situations.

BOOKS

Clicker Training for Dogs, by Karen Pryor, published by Sunshine Books, Inc., June 2002.

Clicking with Your Dog: Step by Step in Pictures, by Peggy Tillman, published by Sunshine Books, Inc., September 2001.

Clicker Training for Obedience: Shaping Top Performance Positively, by Morgan Spector, published by Sunshine Books, Inc., November 1998.

Click for Joy, by Melissa Alexander, published by Sunshine Books, Inc., December 2003.

Clicker Fun: Dog Tricks and Games Using Positive Reinforcement, by Deborah Jones, published by Howlin Moon Press, June 1998.

Dog Whisperer: A Compassionate, Nonviolent Approach to Dog Training, by Paul Owens and Norma Eckroate, published by Adams Media Corporation.

Complete Idiot's Guide to Positive Dog Training, by Pamela Dennison, published by Alpha Books, March 2003.

Dog Friendly Dog Training, by Andrea Arden, published by John Wiley and Sons, Inc., October 1999.

Positive Puppy Training Works: How to Manage, Relate to and Educate Your Puppy, by Joel Walton, published by David & James Publishers, July 2002.

Jelly Bean Versus Doctor Jekyll & Mister Hyde, by C. W. Meisterfeld, published by MRK Publishing, April 1990.

Positive Reinforcement Training: Dogs in the Real World, by Brenda Aloff, published by TFH Publications, Inc., January 2002.

ABC Practical Guide to Dog Training, by Steve Applebaum, published by John Wiley and Sons, Inc., December 2003.

Dog Perfect: The User-Friendly Guide to a Well-Behaved Dog, by Sarah Hodgeson, published by John Wiley and Sons, Inc., May 2003.

How to Say It to Your Dog: Solving Behavior Problems in Ways Your Dog Will Understand, by Janine Adams, published by Berkeley Publishing Group, October 2003.

Back to Basics: Dog Training by Fabian, by Andrea Arden and Fabian Robinson, published by Howell Book House, August 1997.

The Toolbox for Remodeling Your Problem Dog, by Terry Ryan, published by Howell Book House, December 1997.

VIDEOS

As with the books, there are more videos available than I can realistically itemize, so I chose a few that are timely and offer great information while also being entertaining:

The How of Bow Wow: Building, Proofing and Polishing Behaviors, by Virginia Broitman and Sherri Lipman.
This clicker-training video features many important foundation skills that all dogs should learn. It includes advice and tips to help people become better trainers using current shaping techniques showing quick visual progress.

Take a Bow...Wow: Fun and Functional Dog Tricks Video, also by Virginia Broitman and Sherri Lipman.
This video offers a collection of fun and functional dog tricks suitable for assistance-dog training or just plain fun at home. Tricks include ringing a bell to go outside, taking a bow, playing dead, opening and closing doors, waving, chasing his tail and much more. There is also a sequel to this video, *Take a Bow...Wow 2*, that offers more tricks for those who have become fluent with those in the first video.

Click and Treat Training Kit, by Gary Wilkes.
This kit offers a book, video and two clickers and is produced by one of the masters of operant conditioning, Gary Wilkes. He explains how to select, shape and reinforce new behaviors as well as how to anticipate common problems, and he demonstrates practical solutions.

Click and Treat Doggy Repair Kit, also by Gary Wilkes.

This kit includes a video and clicker. It offers the means to overcome destructive behavior using humane and practical techniques. Behaviors addressed include stealing, boundary training, digging, house-soiling, barking, jumping and much more.

Clicker Magic, by Karen Pryor.

This video shows more than 20 actual behavior-shaping sessions, from start to finish. Karen's running commentary explains the skill of pace and timing, and trainers range from total beginners to Karen herself. There's also footage on clicker training cats and fish.

Puppy Love: Raise Your Dog the Clicker Way, also by Karen Pryor.

Ms. Pryor shows how to use clicker training with young puppies to quickly shape appropriate behavior and learn new ones at any age.

Click and Go, by Deb Jones.

This video presents basic principles of clicker training based on sound scientific principles and humane, positive methods. You'll learn how to use clicker-based methods to change your dog's behavior. Techniques include shaping, luring and targeting.

WEBSITES
www.apdt.com

This is the website of the Association of Pet Dog Trainers. This association is geared toward teaching others how to use positive-reinforcement training. Both professional dog trainers and those who only wish to learn how to work with their own dogs are invited to utilize the site's information. From a list of all of the members and means of contacting them to learning how to become a professional trainer and links to more information, this should be a first stop for anyone interested in positive-reinforcement training.

www.wagntrain.com

This site is hosted by Stacy Braslau-Schneck. She offers a plethora of information about operant conditioning, from its history to its current uses. The information will help you understand how this became one of the more widely used training methods as well as how to implement the methods.

www.synalia.com

This site is hosted by Kayce Cover. She is the one who started me on the road to understanding the training process through working with seals and sea lions. She trains Capuchin monkeys to aid the handicapped, and everything from dolphins to dogs using operant-conditioning techniques. Her site has many instructive articles and links, as well as training supplies.

www.canismajor.com/dog/clktrt.html

This site is a dog owner's guide to the click and treat process. Very informative.

www.clickersolutions.com

This site features frequently asked questions about clicker training and helps put everything into perspective. It's a great site for the person who wishes to learn more about clicker training.

www.dog-play.com

This site is hosted by Diane Blackman, who offers many articles about operant conditioning and clicker training.

www.clickandtreat.com

Gary Wilkes's site, which is filled with articles, his seminar schedule and loads of information. He also offers training supplies.

www.clickertraining.com

This is Karen Pryor's site. She offers informative articles, links to locate trainers and information on her seminar and conference schedule, as well as training books and supplies.

www.inch.com/~dogs/clicker.html

The site of the American Dog Trainers Network. You'll spend hours here, as this site is packed with information, links to trainers, links to suppliers and much more.

www.petplanet.co.uk

This site has a great article about how to clicker-train puppies.

www.good-dog-training.com

A site that is filled with articles, links to other sites and supplies.

www.dogwise.com

A site that offers everything you could possibly need to train your dog: books, training supplies, toys and more.

www.sitstay.com

Another site that offers everything you need to train your dog, in addition to many other dog supplies.

www.miriamfields.com

The author's site, includes informative articles, books and supplies (comfort trainer head halter, all-in-one training leash, treat pouch and more).

There are many more sources of information online than what I've listed here. You need only go to these locations and you'll find links to them. The Internet is a goldmine of information. Happy clicking!

INDEX

Adolescent dog 55
Age of dog 51
Aggression 35, 65
Agility 34
Alley Oop 37, 40, 107
Approximation 82
Assertive dog 66
Attention 35, 50, 53
Attentiveness 62
Avoidance 19
Bad habits 34, 108
Barking 17, 24, 117
"Be a Tree" exercise 66
Behavior of Organisms, The 12
Behavior threshold 74
Boredom 79
Break word 53
Breland, Keller and Marian 15
Bridge 19, 20, 74, 104, 111
Bridge/reward 26-28, 34-35
"Bump and Turn" exercise 66
Capturing a behavior 26-27
Chaining 80
Charging up your clicker 28, 57
Chew toys 116, 120
Chewing 24, 116
Choke chain 59
Citronella collar 118
Classical conditioning 15
Clicker training 28, 33, 38-39, 52, 57, 70, 107
—getting started 30
—practicing on a friend 30
Collars 59-61
Combining techniques 35
Come 95, 97
—progressing with distance 98
Command word 54, 58

Consistency 51
Counter-surfing 122
Crate training 109
Crespi 12
Cue word 34
Destructive behavior 108
Digestive system 22, 56
Digging 24
Distance targeting 37
Distance training 76
Distraction-proof 104
Distractions 30, 35, 52, 56
—other dog 102
—working with 59, 101
Dominance 35, 56, 115
Don't Shoot the Dog 28
Down 72
—from a distance 77
—from heel position 74
—with visual cue 74
—with you in varying positions 80
Down-on-the-fly 80-81, 95, 104
Down/stay 89, 95, 106
—moving around your dog 91
Drop-on-recall 81, 95, 104
Electronic training device 65
Electronic-stimulation collar 59, 118
Eliminating bad behavior 108
Enclosed area 38, 51, 100
Ending a session 48, 53, 59
Equipment for target training 38
Escape 19
Excessive barking 117
Extinction 16, 39
Fenced area 38, 51, 100
Fixed interval 16

Fixed ratio 16
Fixed reward 35
Food 20, 22, 26, 32, 35, 56, 62, 65, 68
—drive 27, 51
Garbage can 24, 114
Going-outside behavior 111
Good 40
Head halter 56, 59-60, 65, 122
Heel 55, 58, 71, 80
House-training 108
Ignoring behavior 17
Incorrect response 39
Jumping 17, 112
Keep going signal 25
Kennel up 110
Law of effect 11
Learned response 12
Leash 38, 56, 98, 100, 121
—pulling on 50, 66
—walking 50
Long leash 100
Luring 34-35, 51, 55, 57
—into behavior 26
—into sit 69
—with touch 70
—with toy 69
Marine mammals 15, 31
Martingale collar 59
More than one trainer 22, 45
Motivation 20, 27, 54, 62, 68
Mouthing 115
Negative punishment 17, 19, 34, 56
Negative reinforcement 17, 19, 34, 56, 118
No 23, , 122
No bark collar 118
No response 25
No reward marker 25

Noise box 113, 122-123
Obedience 34
Off-leash recall 100
Off-leash training 51
Older dogs 61
On-leash training 51, 98
Operant conditioning 12, 14-15, 19, 28
Other dog 102
Pattern-trained 79
Pavlov's dog 15
Paying attention 50
Planning a program 45
Positive attitude 111
Positive punishment 17-19, 23, 34, 35, 56, 59, 65, 103-104, 108, 122
Positive reinforcement 15, 17, 19, 22, 34, 35, 56, 62, 117
Praise 26, 33, 51, 65, 68, 107, 111
Prey drive 65
Primary reinforcers 16, 27
Professional trainer 35
Prong collar 59
Pryor, Karen 28, 37, 43
Pulling on leash 50, 66
Punishment 16-17, 46, 103, 108
Puppy attention span 51
Quiet command 121
Random interval 16
Recall 95, 97-98
Redirection 34-35, 121, 123
Regressing 46
Reinforcement 17
Reinforcer 12, 16
Repetition 34, 37, 66, 104
Reshaping behavior 108
Reward 12, 16, 19-20, 22-23, 26, 28, 33, 39, 56, 58, 61, 68, 74, 104, 107, 111
Ringing bell to go out 111

Rushing the door 120
Ryan, Terry 37
Safety 38, 97, 100
Schedules of reinforcement 16
Search-and-rescue 34
Secondary conditioning 14
Secondary negative punishers 23
Secondary positive punisher 23
Secondary punishing reinforcer 56
Secondary reinforcement 16, 33, 40, 103
Secondary verbal punishment 122
Self-rewarding behavior 24, 122
Separation anxiety 117
Shaping a behavior 14-15, 26-27, 31, 33, 41, 51, 82, 111
—practicing on a friend 48
—ten laws 43
Short time spans 53, 107
Sit 68
—from a distance 77
—while heeling 71
Sit/stay 77, 83, 95, 106
—while moving around your dog 88
Skinner Box 12, 31
Skinner, B. F. 12, 15, 17
Sled dogs 50
Spray bottle 113, 122
Stay 82
—and recall 81
—at the door 121
Stealing objects 114, 119
Stimuli 14, 17
Submissive behavior 72
Successive approximation 28, 32, 43, 82

Targeting 36
—at a distance 37
—on hand 36
—on objects 39
Target stick 37-38, 40, 107
—getting started 38
Temperament testing 61
"Ten Laws of Shaping" 43
Thorndike, Edward 11
Throwing out behaviors 22, 25
Timing 19, 25, 30
Tolman, Edward 12
Tone of voice 32, 39
Tool Box for Remodeling Your Problem Dog 37
Touch 26, 32-33, 62, 65, 68
Touch command 40
Toy 26, 35, 68, 116, 119
Training collars 59, 61, 65
Treats 38
"Turn and Redirect" exercise 66
Turning on leash 55, 59
Using techniques correctly 25, 35
Value of reward 20, 54
Variable interval 16
Variable ratio 16, 45
Variable reward 35
Verbal cue 34
Visual signal 34
Voice 39
Walking on leash 50
Watson, John Broadhus 11
Wilkes, Gary 36-37, 39
Work drive 65
Working with distractions 58
Yard 38, 51, 100
Yes 40

Kennel Club Books®

The pet-book authority, Kennel Club Books is currently producing the

WORLD'S LARGEST SERIES OF DOG-BREED BOOKS,

including individual titles on 377 different dog breeds, representing every American-Kennel-Club-recognized breed as well as many other rare breeds for which no titles currently exist in English.

Each Kennel Club Breed Book is at least 158 pages, completely illustrated in color, with a hard-bound cover. The prestigious roster of authors includes world authorities in their breeds, as well as famous breeders, veterinarians, artists and trainers.

Explore the world of dogs by visiting kennelclubbooks.com on the Web and find out more about available titles on fascinating pure-bred dogs from around the globe.

Kennel Club Books, LLC
308 Main Street, Allenhurst, NJ 07711 USA
(732) 531-1995 • www.kennelclubbooks.com